Inner Healing
The Miracle on Goldweber Avenue

Pamela Kennedy

LASER **PRESS**
Publishers
Cinnaminson, New Jersey

Cover illustration by Michael D. Heil

Copyright © 1993 by LaserPress

Library of Congress Catalog Card Number: 93-77671

ISBN 0-9628088-2-2

First printing August, 1993
Printed in the United States of America
Published by Laser Press Publishers, 3005 Waterford Drive, Cinnaminson NJ 08077-4443 Telephone 609-829-3794

In memory of
James P. Lynch
who although ill, by freely opening his home,
made it possible for us to find within ourselves
the beauty of Christ.

ACKNOWLEDGMENTS

I wish to express deep appreciation to:
• **My mother and father** whose prayers have sustained me throughout my life.

• **My friends** who have offered spiritual support and encouragement.

• **Father Brendon Williams, Betty Gene Hickey, and Margaret Lynch** who helped in the production of my manuscript.

•**Joseph Kruger** who advised me on Scripture interpretation.

FOREWORD

by Reverend Brendan Williams

Father Williams is Pastor of the Roman Catholic parish of Saint Veronica, in Howell, New Jersey, and for over four years was the author's counselor and spiritual director.

Over the last twenty years, I have come to appreciate more and more the wonder of Jesus' healing love. The Scripture that describes Jesus as bringing liberty to captives has taken on a deeper meaning for all who have been privileged to witness the marvels of divine love unfold in their lives.

It is the love of Jesus that breaks the bondage of sin. It is His love that protects His children from the cunning prowler and delivers them from Satan's grasp. It is the love of the Sacred Heart that burns away debilitating fears, guilt and anger of the deep unconscious and opens hearts that are broken and empty to new life, a new freedom, a sense of worth, a sense of trust. It is this overflowing love that empowers us to accept and love ourselves and to discover a whole new life in our relationship with our Savior and with His body, the church.

The pages of this book are a testimony to the wonderful love of Christ, which in a very profound way has called Pamela out of her brokenness into the wonderful light of his love. In these pages she invites us on a very intimate journey with her through the dark valleys of bitterness and despair, the perilous byways of addictive behavior, the quaking and treacherous bridges of unwholesome sexual relationships, the quicksand of Satan's deceptions. She leads us with her as she scales the precipice of wholeness. At times it seems an impossible task, filled with anxious moments, but she found the golden rope that was lowered to her by the Lord in His own loving encounter and in the persons of some wonderful Christians who were always there for her. They helped her keep her eyes on Jesus and on the path He had prepared for her. They were strength, encouragement, an arm to rest on, a shoulder to cry on. What a wonderful gift is the body of Christ!

It has been my privilege to have been part of this journey for over four years. During that time, I have seen emerge a loving prayerful person of deep faith, whose spiritual powers have been tempered by the Spirit with the fire and quench-waters of spiritual and emotional struggle. Time and time again Pamela has been forced to reach out and find the tender yet powerful arm of Christ to lead her through as she encountered yet another level of her own frailty and limitation.

This is a story of victory and a message of hope for all who read it. It is Good News in action; it is Jesus' redeeming love enfleshed. It is a shout from the house top that a soul has been saved, a prisoner set free, a person has been reborn, a messenger sent, a disciple empowered. A glowing light has been lit, and it will not be put under a bushel basket. May the beautiful gift of Pamela's life touch all who read these pages and may they be enriched as I have been by walking this journey with her.

CONTENTS

INTRODUCTION

I was the only lesbian among the twelve members of the Inner Healing group that the Spirit gathered in Margaret's house on Goldweber Avenue. Even so, my problems, as you will later see, went well beyond sexual orientation. All the members of our group craved healing for something: rifts between generations, festering emotional wounds from child abuse and incest, alcoholic families, loveless rearing, bad images of God, and terminally ill mates. The consolation of Christ in Inner Healing fits many needs. All of us were hurting, but, in Christ, we were able to pray for and to help each other.

As for myself, I did not discover that I was lesbian until after I was married. When I did, I found a relationship with another woman could be more satisfying than I had ever experienced with a man. A powerful bonding made subsequent fallings-out painful. Many gays sincerely believe they are born that way. I feel homosexuality is acquired; I am convinced in my case it was.

From my own experiences and associations, I do know

1

homosexuals that are neither happy nor proud. Such a life-style can lead to fanatical possessiveness and degradation, and (in spite of the significant accomplishments of activists, in making the world more tolerant and understanding), to low self-esteem, and feelings of guilt and depression. Of my two closest gay friends, one committed suicide; the other died of AIDS. I flirted with suicide, during my own dark night.

Though, as in my case, many homosexuals are dissatisfied with their life-style, they seem unable to change it. I do not judge or condemn them. But to those who have found themselves repeatedly unfulfilled in their life-style, who have exhausted their resources, and have still failed, I would like to tell that there is still hope of finding a more perfect love. When I entered the Lamb of God Prayer Community, (a Catholic charismatic group) I was loved into the kingdom of God.

The Baptist, Episcopalian, and Catholic denominations that planted, watered and fed my faith taught that an active homosexual life-style is sinful. Many homosexuals, in spite of their strong desire for a closer relationship with God, thus, distance themselves from religion. They fear, (and some of them may have even experienced) wrath, rejection, and condemnation. In the charismatic community, without anybody's need to mollify Christian moral precepts, I experienced no wrath, rejection or condemnation, only the unconditional love that Jesus has for all of us. In the inner healing experience that followed it, through the love of others who make up His mystical body, I was able to make dramatic changes in my life. God lifted me from my affliction.

Is Inner Healing for you? Let me tell you my story,

then listen to the Spirit who speaks from within. The way I traveled wasn't always joyful and the spiritual surgery it required wasn't without pain. Sometimes I felt lonely, but I had many friends. My transformation back into the image in which I was made took many tiny steps and many passing seasons; still, it was His miracle— a quiet little miracle among friends in the home of a friend— a miracle on Goldweber Avenue.

The house on Goldweber Avenue (© 1993 by M. Kathleen Tracy. Used with permission.)

PART ONE

THE RETURN OF THE PRODIGAL

This is the story of my life. If you know where I have been, you will more easily vibrate with the feelings I had as Christ hugged me during my Inner Healing. In Part Two, I will share with you some of my best-remembered Inner Healing experiences.

PAINS OF CHILDHOOD

In sharing events from my childhood all facts may not be accurate; they are, however, perceived through the eyes of a child, as true an account as I can give.

In Corning, New York, on May 28, 1942 at 1:30 A.M., I was delivered into this world. I'm told I wasn't a very pretty baby, for I was born without hair, eyelashes, finger nails or toe nails; but they say that beauty lies in the eye of the beholder and my mother saw God's beauty within me.

My new family included a brother Edward who was seven years of age and a sister Ida who was a year and eight days older than I. My birth name was Pamela.

My mother and father were both Protestants and very active in the First Baptist Church. They each had a strong faith in God, so from the beginning our family was rooted in Christian Principles.

I believe my very first emotion was fear. I used to spend much of my time dreading going to bed at night because I was so afraid of the dark. The summer season used to bring some relief, for I was able to catch lightening bugs and for a time they lighted up my room. Naturally I treasured each bug that I found, but I learned quickly that, when concealed in a jar, their life span is short. To this day I still don't know what frightened that tiny child within me, but I do know that I endured terrible fear in that room.

The next fear I was to encounter was of my mother. She was the authority figure in our family. One day while my brother, sister and I were playing, an argument developed over a pencil. My mother heard us arguing and promptly got a branch from her lilac bush, punishing each of us one by one. This was my first experience with discipline. I had never seen my mother react in such a stern and aggressive manner. For a time the relationship between my mother and myself became estranged.

I discovered the fear of being hurt next. Our home was located in the middle of a hill. One day my friend and I journeyed to the top of the hill and we were met by a gang of boys bearing sticks. I don't really know just how long they held us there, but to me each moment seemed endless. When I look back on that incident today, I really believed they were going to harm us. People often say that children have a vivid imagination, but to a child who fears, an imagination has no bounds. As we started back down that hill that day, I took with me a negative image: boys are cruel and not to be trusted.

I started school at the age of five and had no problems with kindergarten or the first grade. By this time my grandfather had become an important part of our lives, and one of the things he used to do was encourage us to get good grades. Report cards soon became a joyful occasion for every "A" brought fifty cents, and every "B" a quarter.

In the second grade my marks took a sharp drop; I began to fail. Failing would mean letting my parents down, my grandfather down, and most of all myself down. This was a difficult learning experience for me because I began to know what it meant to feel inferior to others.

I thought about this situation quite awhile before I received my next report card, and I decided to alter my grades. Giving little thought to the dishonesty of it, I changed the card. I remember meeting my father for lunch and telling him how sloppy the teacher had been with the marks that term. Dear old dad bought my story, but my mother, of course, did not.

Facing my grandfather and my mother was one thing, but facing my school principal was another. I was alone and filled with fear the day she called me in. She questioned me at length, but I continued to maintain that someone else had changed those grades. I left there that day believing that I was a disappointment to everyone, for this was the first time I felt the shame of my own failure.

The year continued and somehow I managed to pass, but not without a change in personality. I had now begun to imitate the speech of other children. First I developed a slight southern accent, and then I began to curse. I soon discovered that cursing was not acceptable either in my home or at the neighbors. Often I was sent home and, of course, I was punished. Now I had no way to vent my anger, for cursing had been my outlet throughout the year. Very soon, seeds of resentment started to take root in my life.

Now I was getting a little older and my brother was starting to take an interest in me. The day came when he decided to teach me how to ride his bicycle. True, I was scared but not enough to pass up a chance like this. He took me down to the alley, set me on his bike, walked with me for awhile, and then he turned me loose. Oh, what an exciting day this was, for up until now I had really accomplished very little. I was so proud of myself that I just couldn't wait to get home and tell my parents. Needless to say, now I wanted a bike of my own. My mother and father agreed that I could have one and so the bicycle was ordered.

It seemed like the day would never come. I had talked about it; I had dreamed about it, and finally the morning arrived. The bicycle was delivered and I was overjoyed. Imagine me having a brand new shiny bike! Without a doubt this had to be the greatest day of my life, or so I thought.

It didn't take long for my parents to discover that the bicyle delivered was much too big for me. In despair I watched out the window as my family made decisions, and within a short time my dream was shattered. The new bicycle was rolled away and soon replaced with my aunt's used one. I can't begin to tell you how deceived I felt. This was my bike; I had dreamed about it, I had planned for it, and no one had a right to own it. The hurt I felt within was unbearable. Feeling like I could trust no one, I struggled alone with this pain. The next day life went on as usual, but in the memory of a small child would remain the gift that had been taken away.

When I was seven years old, my mother decided that

we were going to move to a lovely country home in the town of Big Flats. The property had a lot of land and a fresh running trout stream.

Now taking on a project like this with both parents working and having three small children to care for, would seem like an almost impossible task, but not to my mother. She was determined, and she always accomplished what she set out to do. Within a few months the new house was purchased; the old house was sold; she got her driver's license and bought a car.

I think the hardest thing for her to do was tell my grandfather. We had lived across the street for several years and he had grown very fond of us. It wouldn't really be easy for any of us to part, but eventually we bid farewell and with his blessing we left the house on the hill. As we drove away I found mixed feelings stirring within me. I guess, up until now, things hadn't really been all that bad. I had had a few bouts of sickness, a few run-ins with my mother and a broken arm from a biking mishap.

Now starting to feel a bit sentimental, I thought of all the Memorial Day parades my dad had taken us to and the Denison Park pool that perhaps I would never see again. As Corning faded into the shadows of yesterday, I felt a spark of hope for a better life, yet a sadness for the good memories and people I had to leave behind.

I loved our new home. It was bright and cheery and all on one floor. There were only three bedrooms and that meant my sister and I would share one. Without having to fear the dark, I could relax in the daytime knowing I would be safe at night.

In the beginning our creek was a wonderful advantage. It gave my sister and me a swimming pool and my brother a place to spear fish. Soon we had many friends, and the sound of laughter overflowed its banks.

The first year was a good one for me. My mother had left her job and was now home full time with us. I can recall how great it was getting off the school bus and finding her there to greet us. I loved having her home for it gave me a real sense of security, especially in a strange environment.

When I entered the fourth grade my world slowly began to crumble. I had been having swollen glands and sore throats for quite some time. One day I was rushed to the hospital and the doctor advised my parents to have my tonsils removed. Although I was frightened, the operation went well and I returned home quickly. I wasn't home long when I began to hemorrhage.

I can still remember seeing all the blood upon my pillow. How terribly frightened I was! I was rushed back to the hospital, only this time my stay was much longer. I don't suppose that anyone thought I would live, and least of all myself. I was given a blood transfusion to replace all the blood that I had lost. I was extremely ill, then slowly restored to health.

My mother had now made a decision to go back to work. I guess with all the medical expenses, my family needed the extra paycheck. This was a real setback for me, because I was used to having my mother at home.

At this point my brother became our babysitter. Oh, it was fun for awhile because my brother really had a special knack for entertaining us. So, although I was lonely, I was adjusting well to my mother working again.

One day while my sister and I were at school we were

both called into the office. The principal told us that my mother had had an accident on the way to work and that she had been hospitalized. I could never begin to put into words what I felt in the moments that followed, except to say that I was devastated. Once again the secure little world I had built around me was crumbling. We were sent that afternoon to stay with family friends until they could find someone to take over my mother's duties. Soon they found a replacement, Naomi, one of my mother's closest friends. I had always loved her in the past, but now I was starting to resent everything she did. After all, she wasn't my mother and she had no right trying to take her place.

Filled with resentment, I began to experience real anger and soon I was taking out my hostility on others. I began to turn this anger inward, which caused me to feel soiled and unclean way down deep inside. My mother came home in a short time, but not to the same child she had left behind. I would never again feel secure, knowing that the foundation of my world could be pulled out from under me at anytime.

The next change in my personality was the desire to wear boys' clothing. Up until now my mother had dressed my sister and me very much alike. Our hairdos were usually the same and our dresses often identical. Now I no longer wanted to look like my sister, and least of all like a little girl. My new wardrobe consisted of cowboy boots, a cowboy hat, a gun and a pair of boys sneakers. I'm sure it wasn't easy for my mother to understand that her little girl was choosing a boy's identity.

Recognizing the change in me, my mother tried in different ways to make things better. First she got me a police dog; the dog attacked my girlfriend's lamb. In a few days the lamb died and the dog was taken back to its original owner.

The next thing she did was rent me a trombone. I was thrilled with that, for I was the only girl in Big Flats taking trombone lessons. Eventually I lost interest and the trombone was returned.

My mother then bought me another dog and we named him Coco. What a loving puppy he was! I became attached to him quite quickly; then one day I found that Coco was missing. I called my mother at work but she would give no clues to the disappearance of Coco. That night my mother told us how she had accidentally run over Coco while backing out of the driveway. She had buried him before she left for work. Today I can imagine how difficult that was for her, but back then I only felt the pain of another disappointment and the end of another broken dream.

By now I was in need of some real physical attention. My mother had made several attempts to satisfy me in other ways, but each attempt had failed. What I needed was someone to spend time with me, someone to hold me, and most of all someone to tell me that things would be all right. This request would be a tall order to fill in my house, for each family member seemed to be living his own separate life. No one really had any extra time to take care of someone else's problems. My mother certainly didn't; she had all she could do to work and care for a family of five. My father, although warm and loving, was often unaware of our individual needs. My brother and sister seemed quite well adjusted, and both very busy with their own activities. So, there was really no one who could give me a whole lot of attention.

In our household, getting attention meant being praised if you were good and disciplined if you were bad, and affection did not surface in between. Once again time passed and the desperate cries of a child's heart went unnoticed.

At the age of ten, my sister was employed to take care of the neighbor's children on Saturdays. One Saturday while I was visiting their home, the older two asked me to go to the barn. While I was out there, they showed me how to smoke a cigarette. Feeling very proud of my achievement, I went into the house to show my sister. Little did I ever think that she would betray me, but she did.

When I got home I knew something was wrong, for my father wasn't his friendly self. I said nothing and went on with my day. That evening, my mother came in from work like a lion. She ordered me to go to my room and remove my clothing. Naturally I got the lilac bush again, but that wasn't the worst of it, for anyone could deal with an old lilac bush. My fear was of the dark and my sister was sent away to a family friend. I had to remain closed up and alone in my bedroom overnight. I'm sure my sister was right to tell my mother about the smoking, but it was years before I trusted her again. I believe the pain of her betrayal was worse than the punishment.

Some weeks later, the barn where I had my first cigarette burned down. My family believed that I had a part in setting that fire, but God knows, I did not! The suspicion about the origin of that fire caused my family much embarrassment. Consequently, my father soon resigned from the local Rotary Club, but in time the incident was forgotten. I continued to grow further and further apart from my family. Perhaps it was lack of attention; perhaps it was a lack of understanding, but whatever it was, it drove me into a world of my own. From this lonliness I eventually began to reach out for friends. Soon the games that children play became a source of love to me. Now I was seeking love wherever I could find it.

The next event to take place in our family life was leaving our country home. The State had notified my parents that a new road was being built on Route 17, and it would require our property.

When I was approaching the sixth grade, we moved to a two-story farmhouse. It must have been difficult for my parents to leave a brand new home, only to take on the responsibility of an old one, but this property did have a shed, a barn and a couple of acres of land. My father had built a stone walk leading up to the front door with flowers planted on each side. Within a few weeks, you would have thought that the Kennedys had lived there forever.

I did not adjust well at all in the sixth grade. I do believe that this was because our new location had moved us right next door to the school. Since my mother's accident, I had never overcome the fear of her being taken away from me. My mother drove to work four days a week with passengers, but Friday was her day to drive alone. I don't know why I felt she was always safe, if she had someone with her, but I did. I hated every Friday, for from my classroom window I would watch my mother as she drove away. Then there was the fear, all day long, that the principal would call me in his office to tell me of another accident.

Not knowing how to cope with these feelings or how to

express my fears, I began to do strange things. Each Friday I would go home at lunch time and put on my mother's best clothing. This helped to take my mind off her traveling and somehow got through the day. Eventually it left its mark though, for I started skipping school and before long there was a truant officer at my door. Needless to say, I had to repeat the sixth grade. By now I was beginning to have a severe attitude change and I was very angry, not only on the inside, but also on the outside. Nobody seemed to understand just how depressed I really was. As my life went on, I continued to go downhill.

My mother made desperate attempts to help the situation by adding to my activities Bible camp, 4-H camp, choir, Youth Fellowship and a new bicycle, but all fell short of the affection I was seeking.

Oh, I tried Youth Fellowship for a while and in the beginning it was great. I loved the minister and his wife; I made a few friends, and I was even elected president. Then the Christmas season came and we voted to help the poor during the holidays. Our project was to collect used toys and to restore them either by varnishing or repainting them. While we were out collecting toys one weekend, the cars parked at the American Legion were splashed with paint. It wasn't long before the sheriff was at our minister's house asking to see the inside of the church and the paint we had used for the toys. We were questioned at length and sent home. I could understand their interrogation, for they would certainly have to check out any available lead that involved paint.

When I arrived home that night, I did not mention the incident to anyone. I knew there was no way that I could prove my innocence, so I thought it was best not to mention it at all. I sat quietly, but panic stirred deep within me. A little while later, my brother came barging into the living room, demanding to see my hands. This hurt me deeply for I couldn't believe my brother would ever think that I could do such a thing as to use church paint to damage property. My response was now anger, unlike other incidents when my brother had provoked me to sadness or fear. Then I was remembering back to the fire in the barn when he neglected to clarify that I was with him when the fire started. Why didn't he defend me then and why was he accusing me now? At a time like this, I really needed the support of a big brother but he gave none. In attempting to prove my innocence, I called on the sheriff at his home. He neither believed me nor encouraged me to pursue my own defense. So I let the issue drop, but the memory of being falsely accused lingered on.

Months later, my brother had an errand to do at the church hall and he asked me to go with him. I followed him from room to room, and as we entered the last room, I happened to notice the Sunday School money was still on the tables. My brother remarked about it and then we left.

I never thought anymore about this until it was near Valentine's Day. I was in a store buying something I needed when I saw some expensive candy hearts. I thought of the teachers who might love me if only I could give them such a gift, but I knew of nowhere to get money. Oh, I had an allowance but that was a dollar a week and these were five dollars apiece. I knew when I left that store that I had to have those hearts. That night as I lay in my bed, I remembered all the Sunday School money left on the tables. My first instinct, having been raised a Christian. was "Oh you can't do that",but then I thought of all the love I would receive and so it seemed worth the risk.

The side door of the church was off the main street, and there was very little traffic that came that way. Picking a lock was not so easy but once I learned how, it changed my life. The teachers I bought the hearts for seemed to take notice of me after that. They would smile when I walked in their rooms and they began to ask me to do little favors that they didn't ask others to do. For the first time I was getting attention and I loved it. Even my classmates who used to harass me I no longer had to fear for now I was able to treat them at the local soda bar. This was another time I found myself violating the Christian principles I had been taught.

I never realized the tremendous impact my brother had made on my life until he left for college. I guess up until then I always took him for granted. My brother never showed any outpouring of emotions while he was growing up, and so I learned to keep my feelings for him well hidden. I suppose our age difference had a great deal to do with it but, what ever the reason, I had never discovered the depth of my love for him.

When my brother left home, he was everything I wanted to be. He was male; he was successful and he was the apple of my mother's eye. There was no room in my heart for jealousy, for he was my big brother and I was proud of him.

Saying our goodbyes at Mansfield State College, in Pennsylvania, was a very sad day for me. The emotions

I was experiencing that day were not the feelings I was prepared to deal with. My family seemed to handle the situation well and soon carried on with their lives. I was expected to do the same.

The first few months of his absence, whenever I found time to be alone, I cried. I found comfort within my tears, for they became an expression of healing as well as an outlet for my feelings.

As time passed I began to have many depressing moments without him. I felt he had abandoned me and I was beginning to feel very insecure. Now all of a sudden I realized how little I had appreciated him, and just how much he really meant to me. I grieved for him quite awhile, and when I could tolerate the hurt no longer, I buried my pain.

I didn't know much about praying then, but I was told that God hears the prayers of every child and so I began to pray for my brother. My brother is a minister today, and I believe that those same prayers helped lead him safely through college and seminary.

In my early teens there were also some moments of happiness, for my grandfather purchased land on Waneta Lake. The day I heard the news I was excited, for until then I had been seeing him only on holidays and occasionally on a Saturday. As my mind wandered back to Corning, I could still remember how close we used to be. Perhaps now we would have time together to rekindle that love.

I took awhile to clear the land, but everybody pitched in and soon the lot was bare. The cottage was a one floor dwelling built of cinder blocks. It was really a joy to see the family work together; there was a feeling of happiness in the air. Within a few weeks a dock was built and a motor boat was launched.

I couldn't begin to tell you what all this meant to me, after the many disappointments I had experienced. Now I would get the opportunity to spend my summers with my grandfather.

From then on it was truly a learning experience for me, as my grandfather never took "No." for an answer. I learned to catch fish, how to kill and clean them, and how to steer and dock a boat. I'm sure I was one of the youngest navigators on Waneta Lake.

One of the greatest things about my grandfather was his honesty. I always knew just where I stood with him, for he never pulled any punches. If I made him angry he became very quiet, and if I pleased him his smile would warm my day. His love was always genuine and always freely given. He didn't show a lot of physical affection, but he shared his heart and that was good enough for me.

My grandfather was a very positive influence and, although his influence did not change the course of my life, it set examples that I was to follow in years to come. Through his disappointments he taught me to have hope, for even on our darkest days God can send forth a rainbow. In his love he taught me to seek the beauty of the earth; only then will we find the peace and contentment we desire. By his faith he taught me that, if I make God my constant companion, no matter how rough the road becomes, every moment of life is worth living.

The day did come when the cottage became only a memory, but I never did forget the love that was shared on Waneta.

I remember how excited I was when I was transferred

to Horseheads Junior High, knowing for the first time in my life I was really going to be a "big shot". I felt the change would be good for me, having a new environment and all new teachers.

I made lots of friends in the first year, attended the school dances and, although it was an effort, I somehow managed to pass. In the eighth grade I was not as successful, for my sister had already set a precedent and the teachers expected as much from me as they had received from her. My joy soon turned to anger and I became indifferent to school. My grades were failing that year but my mother persuaded the principal to promote me, and so I was moved into High School.

The ninth grade was a real struggle for me. I tried hard to achieve good grades and once again I failed, but the year wasn't a total loss for a young man had entered my life. He was older than myself and worked as a farm hand at one of the local dairys. He had an easy going personality, freely spending the money in his pocket, and he had a car to travel around in. Although he wasn't the answer to my quest for love, he filled my well of lonliness and so we became constant companions.

Again I was to experience the humiliation of repeating a grade. Now with little hope of ever graduating, I decided to leave both home and school. One day I arranged for my boyfriend Ronnie to pick me up at school during my lunch break. I knew my parents were both working, so I had nothing to worry about. We returned to my home in Big Flats and went in the house together. Within a short time, practically everything I owned was in Ronnie's car.

The first night we slept in the car, but by the second

night we had located friends in the New York City area. They was glad to see us and and willing to let us stay; however, by that evening my mother had tracked us down. We were ordered to come home at once and I needn't tell you how frightened we were.

When we arrived in Big Flats, my mother was at the door to meet us. Entering the house again with all my clothes was a very difficult thing to do. My mother had little to say to me, and she ordered Ronnie to leave, forbidding him to visit again. I was back in school the following Monday.

Now totally unhappy, I started associating with an older crowd at school. They seemed to enjoy my laughter and invited me to all their parties. My girlfriend Ginny lived in a converted pool room with her family, and although it was off limits to me, I started hanging out there also. My mother disapproved of these people, and so did most of the local townspeople. I suppose it was because the pool hall had always had a bad reputation, and this family had now purchased it for a residence, They soon became known as "the pool room gang". Little did anyone know what good people they really were.

I was delighted to have new friends and would sneak into their home every opportunity I found. As big as I was Ginny's mother sensed my need for love and, when ever I went there, she would take me on her lap and rock me. I believe this was the first physical attention I ever remember receiving. This woman's love was to bring about another change in my life, for now I was beginning to desire affection from females rather than from males. I continued to date boys, but something had changed within me.

In the middle of my teens I met some people who were Baptists,from the church next door to ours. They invited me to attend one of their services and my mother gave her permission. I had expected this church to be similar to our church, but it wasn't. The members of our church were always very devoted, but there was something different about these Baptists. They seemed to generate love and they all were on fire for the Lord. I had never seen such happiness. Indeed they had something special and I knew, regardless of what it would require, I wanted it.

Approaching my mother about leaving our church was difficult, but I took the risk. To my surprise she granted my wish and I joined the neighborhood Baptist church. Within a year I was baptized by immersion and started to live what I thought to be a new life.

I became very active in Youth Fellowship on Sundays and the Bible Study on Wednesday nights. In the summer of that year the church ran a contest called "Saving Souls for Jesus". The winner of the contest was to be awarded an airplane ride, with the minister, over Harris Hill. I brought several friends with me to the service, including the family from the pool hall, some of them received the Lord. I won the contest and in the fall I took my first airplane ride.

Then one day during the morning worship, the minister announced that the sermon he had prepared would be changed due to a knock that had come on his door in the middle of the night. The pool hall was directly across the street from the parsonage, and there had been an accident in the middle of the night claiming the lives of two people. One of them was my dear friend Ginny.

At that moment I was overwhelmed with grief. I sat dazed throughout the sermon and left the church in a state of shock. This was my first experience with death, and I really didn't know how to cope with it. In the weeks that followed I was once again facing lonliness, fear and anger. In my sorrow there was no one to turn to, so I buried my grief and walked on. A few weeks later I returned to the pool hall where Ginny had lived, but it was never the same without her.

Now at the age of seventeen my world began to crumble once again. The church that had become so meaningful in my life was no longer important to me. I am sure that Ginny's death had taken its toll on my spirituality. I started smoking cigarettes soon after that. Eventually I dropped out of school and my aunt hired me as a full-time babysitter. By this time my mother was becoming very alarmed, for I had no interests and no goals. She arranged for me to see a psychiatrist in Elmira. While this doctor was questioning me, I was terrified, fearing insanity and the possibility of being committed to a state hospital. The doctor sent me home with medication, but this did not change my behavior.

Because the psychiatrist could give no explanation, my mother sought a physical diagnosis. I was hospitalized and tested for brain abnormalities. The test consisted of injecting air into the spine to Xray my brain. I was a week in the hospital with excruciating pain and severe nausea. The results of the test were negative and the only diagnosis was malnutrition. I was sent home.

Soon after my hospitalization, my sister graduated from Horseheads High School. I attended her graduation and found it to be a very painful occasion. As she went forward for her diploma, the early years of our lives began to surface in my memory. Before we moved to Big Flats my sister and I had been inseparable.

As I watched in tears while she walked across the stage, I wondered where all those years between Big Flats and Corning had gone. How proud I was to see her in her cap and gown, yet saddened to know that she too was now college bound. As sisters we had had our ups and downs, but in my heart I had always loved her. Her going away would certainly leave a tremendous void in my life.

Home was no longer the same without my sister. It seemed strange sitting down to the dinner table without her, and the bedroom we had shared now seemed so empty. However, I continued to babysit and time traveled on. I had been dating Ronnie since we ran away together. Now, in order to make my own decisions and lead my own life, I felt that marrying Ronnie would be my only alternative. So at the age of eighteen, I left my childhood behind to become Mrs. Ronald Murphy.

PART ONE: CHAPTER TWO

BATTLE WITH SATAN

In this chapter, names have been changed to protect the identity of some individuals described

From the very beginning our marriage was a disaster. My wedding night was certainly not an occasion that anyone would ever want to remember.

I was married in the evening in a small country church up in the hills. I wore for my wedding dress a green woolen jumper and a long sleeved yellow blouse. There were no flowers, no music and no guests. My family refused to attend and we invited no friends other than a married couple who were our witnesses. The minister was very brief; our vows were exchanged quickly and we left.

My first home was a rented trailer in the village of Horseheads. Ronnie found a job on a nearby farm and I attempted to become a housewife. Within a few weeks I found that I had little interest in cooking or cleaning. I also realized that I was homesick, especially for my father.

Although my father never really understood my fears or the problems I endured as a youngster, he still seemed to be there in other ways for me. True, he was not the father figure that one would expect, but he did become my closest buddy throughout my childhood.

He always had a positive attitude and his joyful personality was the only real source of laughter in our home. So naturally I was drawn to him. We seemed to have a bond, and that, I believe, was the spirit of Christ within each of us. We often shared the same interest which made this bond even stronger. My father liked to plant and garden and so did I. Together we planted seeds that grew beautiful flowers and a garden that grew healthy vegetables. We each took an interest in raising animals, so our back yard coop was filled with chickens and rabbits.

Now I was remembering back to when housework was a pleasure because I shared it with him. My father was a very musical man and his music turned housework into moments of joy. If he wasn't singing Christian tunes, then he'd be playing his spoons.

Sharing household chores with him over the years had really been festive occasions. With all these joyful memories, I was now beginning to miss him terribly. His joy was not in my home nor was his laughter, and housework was no longer fun without him.

Consequently, I began to spend my afternoons in a local bar. It was exciting for a while, having freedom and little responsibility, but soon I became restless and encouraged Ronnie to move on.

Our next home was in Canton, Pennsylvania. Ronnie

had managed to save some money, so we purchased a small trailer and had it moved to his family's property. This move proved to be a big mistake for his family, like mine, had always been opposed to our marriage. I was hoping that perhaps, given enough time, their opinion of me might change, but it did not. I had no alternative now but to try to make the best of a stressful situation. In the months that followed I put my best foot forward, but I always encountered rejection. It wasn't long before I began to have real bouts of depression.

Ronnie was unable to find a job, so our funds were running low. The only available work in town was collecting horse manure from the stables and selling it to the local farmers for fertilizer. If there was any pride left within me from my family roots, it soon fell by the wayside, for pitching horse manure became our daily routine.

My depression continued and I began to experience moments of lonliness, but this time at a much deeper level than I had ever experienced before. Having no one else to turn to, I reached out to a woman I had met in a bar.

At first sharing our afternoons together was a lot of fun. Lisa had a gift of laughter and an understanding heart to comfort me on my down days. Little did I realize just how attached I was becoming to her until one evening, feeling especially discouraged, I took the car and headed for the village.

When I arrived at the bar, Lisa greeted me with a friendly hello but gave no indication of wanting me to join her. I watched in anger as she made her advances towards the male customers. Feelings of possession were now entering my world, for she was my friend and no one else had a right to share her company. Devestated, I began to drink quite heavily and by the end of the evening had to be carried out of the place.

By the time Ronnie got me home I was fully conscious and very angry. Normally I did not express anger but that evening, feeling totally betrayed, I broke most of the dishes in my kitchen. The next day, broken hearted inside and understanding little of what was going on within me, I convinced Ronnie that Canton was no longer the place for me. I encouraged him to enlist in the Army and I returned home to live with my family.

Ronnie had been gone a year when I met an older man who promised me the world. Dave was twenty years older than I, married and the father of three. He had money; he liked to drink and he loved to dance. His gentle manner and quiet humor won my heart so we began to date. His personal life did not appear to affect his work or his lifestyle, so we pretended his marriage did not exist.

We dated for quite awhile before Dave was transferred down South. After a couple of months he asked me to join him and I flew South. He provided a motel room for me in a town near his work. Then one day I received a call from his wife, informing me that although she was in a different state she was aware of what was going on. She requested that I leave immediately and so I returned home the very next day.

Now I wondered how I was ever going to face Ronnie again, and did I really even want to. I was no longer the innocent young girl that he had married for I had violated the sacred vows of matrimony.

In the South I had learned to abuse the use of alcohol. Even Sundays, which had always been sabbath days for me, had now become days for shooting dice in someone's living room, and always with a few drinks. I tried to justify my behavior by remembering the many times I had pleaded with Ronnie to root our marriage in the foundation of the church. Perhaps he would be happier now that I had become so engrossed in the world. Regardless of what he might feel, there would be no turning back for I had sold my values for the high price of freedom.

After living home a short while I met another man. He was free; he had never been married; he had no children, and he had a very good job. Before long we were considering Nevada as a possibility for my divorce and then wedding plans in the near future.

We decided to purchase our home first before flying to Nevada, so I left my parents' home and moved in. He remained in his apartment.

Soon I began to drink more frequently. Perhaps it was out of lonliness, or perhaps it was just boredom, but whatever it was, it eventually led to our separation.

When Sam found out how much I was drinking he called my mother requesting that I be removed from his trailer. I felt very betrayed, and once again was forced to return home. Living at home this time did not last long because I was unable to conform to their way of life. Now trusting no one, I continued on my path of destruction.

Since my family was thoroughly disgusted with me, I now made the bars my home base. I spent my time playing shuffleboard and poker to supplement my allotment check. By midnight I was usually intoxicated and often went home with regular customers.

This horrendous lifestyle continued for several months. Meanwwhile I managed to handle a part time job which gave me the funds to buy a used car. From then on, I often slept in my own car.

As I look back on this experience today, I know that God surely sent His angels to protect me. I was never mistreated and I was never molested. Although I was of drinking age, through God's grace, people were able to view me as a child.

My bar career came to a halt when my grandfather attempted to salvage my life. I had applied for a job in Corning Hospital as a nurse's aide and was hired, so my grandparents decided I should live with them. Soon I had made a few friends and joined a women's bowling league.

After I had bowled for while, I began to sense that there was something very different about the women on my team. It was really nothing that I could define, but yet something I could feel.

Then one night while my car was in the garage for repairs, a woman called Bess offered to drive me home. She asked if I would mind going for a ride with her. I could see that she was indeed troubled, so I agreed to go. We drove a few miles out of town. Then all of a sudden she pulled off the highway into a deserted parking area near the river. She then came to an abrupt stop. Within a few minutes she began to speak. I listened as she struggled to find the words to tell me about her life.

She was a lesbian; she had been been married, was now separated and living alone with her only son. She told me that she had been a very lonely person for a long time and that, since I had joined the bowling team, I had become an important part of her life. She said that over the months she had grown to love me in a very special way.

I cannot begin to tell you what those words meant to me, except to say that when I heard them something happened within me. It seemed as if this was the moment I had been waiting for all my life— someone to tell me from their own heart how very much they loved me. Soon there was an exchange of tears and a warm embrace. This union was to bring about the most drastic change ever to take place within me. My relationship with Bess did not last long for she returned to her husband, but it did last long enough for me to discover that a homosexual relationship was far deeper and much more meaningful than any heterosexual relationship that I had ever encountered. Before long, I found myself in another affair, where moments of passion became the fulfillment of love never received.

By now it was time to leave my grandparents, for my lifestyle had changed. I resigned from my job and moved on. Eventually I returned to the bars.

The day came when I was encouraged by an Episcopal priest to do something with my life, so I enrolled in a school of beauty culture. A year later I graduated, took my state boards and opened a small shop in Elmira, New York.

I hadn't felt a strong call from God since I joined the Baptist church as a teenager. Now He seemed to be calling me again, so I took instructions at Grace Episcopal Church and was confirmed. It became very meaningful to me because, for the first time in my life, I could received the sacrament of communion each Sunday.

By now I was so involved in my own life that I had completely forgotten I was a married woman. One day my doorbell rang and it was Ronnie. He had served his time in the Army and was now a civilian again. It was surely an awkward situation, having a friend and a husband under the same roof, but he had no place to live so I allowed him to stay.In time I shared my story with him and somehow he understood. In fact, he blamed himself for refusing to ground our marriage in a Christian foundation.

Later that year my friend Susan, lost her job due to her alcoholism, so I closed my shop. Consequently, the three of us moved on to Spring Valley, New York.

The Valley had many things in store for us, some of which were good and some bad. One of the first events to take place was when my friend Susan decided that she was not a homosexual and therefore she could not continue to live in the manner in which we were living. In a way this proved to be one of the good events, for it gave Ronnie and me a chance to try to restore our marriage. I did remain at Susan's apartment, but we began to live separate lives.

Ronnie and I quit our jobs and trained to become school bus drivers. From then on, we saw each other on a daily basis. Our attempt to put the marriage back together lasted a year, but it was too late; the damage had already been done. Ronnie eventually went back to Horseheads to live, and I remained in Spring Valley with the bus company. I was lonely for a while, but in time I adjusted and began to seek happiness for my life. This time though, I attempted to seek spiritual fulfillment rather than physical pleasures, for once again I was experiencing God's call, so I decided to take instructions in St. Joseph's Catholic Church.

I was baptized* and confirmed, and in the year that followed I tried desperately to live a Christian life. However, my efforts added up to another failure due to the guilt that engulfed me. I did make visits to the confessional for a few months, but soon I was back on the streets, numbing my memories with alcohol.

My next relationship was with a woman named Kim. She was in her late twenties, single and appeared to be quite masculine. Now I had a strong desire to meet her, and a desire to know just who she really was.

One night I took the liberty of introducing myself and Kim and I became close friends. Within a year, we moved in together. Our relationship lasted six years, and it is no stretch of the imagination when I tell you it was a total disaster. I guess having youth on our side helped us to survive, but not without scars.

It wasn't until we were well into our relationship that I discovered Kim had a severe drinking problem. Her drinking progressed to the point that, whenever I would insist she go to bed, an argument would ensue, sometimes bringing with it physical abuse.

Later on in our relationship, Kim landed in the

---

* The Roman Catholic Church currently acknowledges the validity of the sacrament of Baptism as administered by the Baptist and Episcopal denominations. Today, Baptism would not normally be repeated, even on a conditional basis, when such a Christian affiliates with the Catholic tradition.

emergency room for treatment. That night after returning home she had a mild case of the D.T.'s. After that
experience she made a sincere effort to curb her drinking.

The day came when we were offered better jobs in a
state operated nursing home. In the beginning we each
tried hard to fulfill our duties. We were faithful, punctual
and always agreeable.

Then we were taken off the day shift and put on
nights. This turned out to be our downfall, for we were
still weekend drinkers. After two months of the late shift
and only two weekends off, we began to drink in the
daytime. We started calling in sick and soon used up our
allotted days for illness. Consequently, we were both
fired a week before our probation period ended.

Our next stop was the county welfare. We now had no
jobs and no money so they agreed to help us temporarily
until we could get on our feet. Getting on our feet turned
out to be only an expression, for we were never able to
straighten out our lives while we were together

In time I began to feel very dirty about my homosexuality, and so my drinking increased. In an effort to escape
these feelings of uncleanliness, I began to experiment
with drugs. By the grace of God, I discovered quickly that
drugs and alcohol do not mix.

Before our relationship ended, Kim and I were involved in a brawl with two other lesbians, in the lobby of
our apartment house. Kim was badly beaten and taken
by ambulance to the Ramapo General Hospital, and I was
encouraged to go to the police station to press charges
against these women.

Much to my surprise, when I arrived at the police
station I too was arrested and fingerprinted. If I ever

thought in the past that I knew the true meaning of the word betrayal, I was wrong. Never before had I been so deceived! Feelings of hate began to overwhelm me as I stared at this man. I wondered how anyone could be so cruel. This fight was definitely the fault of the other two women, and the policeman knew this.

Within the next hour Kim was brought to the jail in handcuffs. I was heartsick when I saw her. Her face was so badly beaten that she was barely recognizable.

In the morning when it was daylight, they called for a judge. The judge set bail at two hundred dollars each but none of us had the funds to pay it. We were then handcuffed and taken to the county jail.

That evening we were taken to the courthouse. By now my spirit was broken, for the strong walls that I had built around me had been completely destroyed. I entered the courthouse drained of emotion. The many tears that I had shed throughout the day were all gone.

As I walked toward the judge, I spotted my mother. My shame was indescribable. I immediately tried to cover my blood stained coat,but it was virtually impossible for there was just too much that had dried on it from the night before.

Court was adjourned that evening until a later date, for we each needed to retain a public defender. My mother stayed on with us for a few days but then returned home. Kim and I were fortunate for our lawyers turned out to be excellent. Eventually all charges were dropped against us.

We left the valley and moved to my home town in upstate New York. We were both hired in the Corning Glass Works. After being there awhile, Kim found someone she cared for very much, and so she left me. Although it was a blow to my heart as well as my ego, it was time for our relationship to end.

My next relationship was with a much older woman. Alice was divorced; she had a grown son and had been living alone for several years. She worked as a cook six days a week in the town diner. We met in a local bar. We started playing shuffleboard together and before long I had joined her life.

She liked to gamble, so we started going to the race track on weekends. Friday nights became our poker night; Sundays was an euckre game at the neighborhood bar.

Eventually I quit my waitress job and went to work with Alice. We continued to gamble throughout our relationship, but after awhile it was no longer exciting.

In time we both gave up our weekend drinking, for the desire to have fun was gone. We moved to New Jersey but within a few months we each found different interests; our relationship eventually ended.

For the next five years I did not get intimately involved with anyone. Somehow I knew I needed space so, although my search was not yet over, it was something that would have to be put on hold for awhile. Soon I was placed on disability for arthritis and moved to the town of Weehawken. This was a quiet little town, one that drew its source of peace from the banks of the Hudson River, which it overlooked. I especially liked it there for I could see the New York City skyline from my Boulevard East apartment.

I found it comforting to live in a place where race or religion was not an issue. In time I began to mingle and so I made friends of many different nationalities. It was here that I learned a lesson on love and a little more insight into the true meaning of friendship.

After a year I was feeling better, so I applied for a job as a security guard at a college in Jersey City. I worked there three years and then reapplied for disability.

In 1981 I entered into my last homosexual relationship. Her name was Sonia and I met her while she was visiting in Union City. She was married and the mother of four grown children. She and her husband were living together but leading separate lives. Sonia told me that their physical relationship had ceased years ago and that they were now living as brother and sister.

After spending only weekends together for almost a year, Sonia encouraged me to move to Bricktown. My new home was a tiny bungalow next door to Sonia's house. It was adorable and, although small, it was sufficient for my needs.

Sonia was seventeen years older than I and spent much of her time reading and watching television. She also spent time each day preparing meals for the three of us.

Saturday was the designated night given to me, the only time when I would have Sonia's undivided attention. I had developed an interest in camping years ago and had bought a small camping trailer. Once I introduced Sonia to camping she became a real pro. Within a short time she was planning our next weekend at the lake.

Sonia didn't like to be away from home every weekend for, although she and Peter were no longer close, she still felt obligated to be home most to the time. Besides, her children often visited on weekends. I learned to adjust to

Sonia's routine and soon our relationship began to deepen.

About six months after I moved to Sonia's I started to feel ill. I began to go to the doctor complaining of one symptom or another, not knowing how to describe just what was happening to me. My doctor, unable to make a specific diagnosis, suggested several changes in my diet and also prescribed medication. My symptoms continued but they did not seem to interfere with our camping trips.

During the following year two major problems developed, affecting our relationship. The first incident began when Sonia suggested that, rather than paying for storage, I should let her son bring my camper to Bricktown. Soon there was a lot of discord in Sonia's family about the use of the camper. They now wanted it all to themselves. In order to avoid further trouble, I transferred the title to Sonia.

Life returned to normal again until Sonia and I decided to take a vacation. Naturally we wanted to camp, so we were planning to use the trailer. Sonia suggested that perhaps this time we should share our vacation with Peter. Peter decided not to go and instead of making it clear to the family that it was his decision to stay home, he let them believe we were rejecting him. Consequently there was a heated argument between Sonia and her son, and she agreed to leave the trailer behind. We left for our camping trip with only a pup tent and a makeshift screen house. I was livid with anger but determined not to ruin our long awaited vacation. The weather was stormy that week and the winds were strong. We could find no way to secure the tent, so that it was constantly blowing down. I tried hard not to express my feelings, and I tried even harder to convince myself that I was having a good time.

By the middle of the week I realized that something had changed within me, for I no longer respected Sonia's decisions.

In the middle of the week Peter apologized to Sonia over the phone and then arrived to spend the night. I was certainly not happy that she had insisted upon calling him, nor was I delighted at his arrival. Now after causing us disappointment as well as inconvenience, he wanted to invade our vacation. This only enhanced my anger.

Sometime in the night I realized that there was something not healthy nor right about this whole situation. Why did Sonia have to call Peter anyway, when she said they each lived separate lives?

The day we returned home I demanded to know the real nature of her relationship with Peter. Sonia, knowing that she had been caught in her own lie, responded by saying that she had never asked me to live with her, only to come and share her life. Once again I felt betrayed. With a broken heart, I left behind a trailer that I called home and I headed back to Weehawken.

The months that followed were lonely months for me. Sonia called frequently pleading for my forgiveness, but I needed space for myself and time to forgive her.

Eight months later I did return to Bricktown, but this time only as a friend. There could never again be a homosexual relationship between us.

Soon I began to feel ill with the same symptoms that I had had before, only this time they were more intense. Assuming that my arthritis was the direct cause, I continued to push myself, determined not to give in to my illness.

Sonia was also ill and had surgery in November.

Fortunately I had good days as well as bad, so I was able to spend time with her at the hospital.

My left leg had recently been turning outward and by December of that year it was becoming difficult for me to walk. At first the doctor was reluctant to recommend a leg brace, fearing I would become too dependent on it. However he soon recognized my need and ordered it. Getting adjusted to the brace took time, but it was worth the struggle.

In January Sonia had another operation, but this time her recovery was not as speedy. A few days after her discharge she had a seizure. The doctor prescribed dilantin, hoping to prevent further seizures, but he could not be certain if the treatment would be successful.

Peter, now in fear of leaving her alone in the house, asked if I would come and stay with them. I still loved Sonia in a very special way, and, although sick myself, I did want to help. So I packed some clothes and moved next door.

In February I was placed on crutches for a weakness in my right hip, but it did not prevent me from staying with Sonia. Within three months she was stabilized on her medication, and I moved back to the bungalow. Not long after my return, my illness became more severe. The doctor, still not knowing the source, took many tests, sending me from one specialist to another. By fall my symptoms had all increased. The whole right side of my body was now affected by weakness. My eyes felt like sandbags and were swollen each morning. My mouth was filled with ulcers and my legs were doubling up, causing severe pain. The constant diarrhea was depleting a lot of my energy.

I was having difficulty using my arms, so washing, dressing and combing my hair took much effort. My heart was monitored because the palpitations continued.

Eventually new symptoms began to surface such as hallucinations and periods of sweating. My doctors, although completely puzzled, attempted to exhaust every avenue so the evaluations continued.

If I ever felt completely alone in my life, it had to be now. It was here in the middle of my illness that I called on God. How strange that all my life He had been beckoning me and now I was beckoning Him. The thought of dying is a frightening experience when your soul is caught unprepared. In the midst of life the reality of death was now before me, and it was time to make my peace with God. I wondered where I would begin after years of rejecting Him. Would He still listen to the plea of a sinner, and would He still hear the cry of a frightened child?

After years of living in a barren land, I reached for the only thing I thought might help, my Bible. My mother's favorite Psalm was always the twenty third and so I began to read it. "Yea, though I walk through the valley of the shadow of death I will fear no evil, for Thou art with me."* As I read this portion of the Psalm, peace descended upon my broken soul. As I began to weep God flooded this temple with tears of tender mercy. From then on I lived what I thought would be my final days through the voice of scripture.

Each day became a valuable treasure, starting and ending with Him. As I traveled through the stages of preparing for death, God walked with me. Naturally

---

*Authorized King James Version, verse 4.

denial took its toll but, once it was over, I was free to journey spiritually, As I surrendered my life to Him, I began to live each day to the best of my ability. In time I was able to accept my destiny, so I called home asking my parents to purchase my grave.

In the days ahead God sent me a miracle of hope. It is said that if one has faith, hope will follow and it did. Soon a prayer from the heart emerged and I found myself praying to live so that I might serve Him. This prayer continued for nine months.

Unknown to me, a friend of mine was making a novena for my recovery. Early one morning while she was visiting me, God revealed to her that the source of my illness was related to an odor coming from the bungalow.

At my doctor's suggestion my home was tested by a technician from the New Jersey Environmental Control. It was found that carbon monoxide was escaping from the kitchen stove. The state toxicologist ordered me to leave the premises immediately, and my doctor advised me that, as a health precaution, I should no longer live there.

And so my battle with Satan had come to an end. The ugly path of destruction that I had paved so many years ago had now reached its final resting place. Indeed there had been a death, a death of self and a grave to bury the memories of my past. With God's promise of new life and hope for tomorrow, I closed the door of the tiny bungalow.

PART ONE: CHAPTER THREE

SPIRITUAL JOURNEY

The spring of 1985 brought with it a time of prayer and much thanksgiving, a time to reflect on all my many blessings. My new home was a small trailer located in a campground in Jackson, New Jersey. Maple Lake was a peaceful place to live, a place where nature nestled deep within my spirit.

This was truly the perfect setting to recuperate. It took the summer months, a lot of fresh air, and plenty of sunshine before I was able to navigate again. Once the pain in my legs began to ease, I attempted to take short walks daily from my trailer to the lake, hoping that fresh air and exercise would bring a change in my health.

Soon serenity began to fill my weeks, as each day became a day of resting, trusting, and waiting for the Lord. Oh, it is not to say there weren't setbacks as well as disappointments, but somehow I learned to cope with them. By the Fall I was able to walk halfway around the lake, and I was pleased with my progress.

After spending much time alone, I was beginning to

know myself a little better. Throughout my life I had been surrounded with negativity, so I often looked at the dark or downside of everything. Realizing now the toll this illness had taken on my physical body, I knew I would have to surround myself with positive thoughts and positive people, if I were ever going to get well again.

There was a restaurant near the campgrounds that featured Christian music twice a week. It was nondenominational with everyone welcome. Not really knowing in what direction God wanted to lead me, I decided to visit the restaurant, seeking Christian fellowship.

It was wonderful being around a group of people who had made a commitment to follow Christ. Their joy seemed to fill the air as they sang, danced, and praised the Lord. Soon I had an abundance of Christian friends. They all had positive attitudes about their daily lives, knowing that God would supply their needs.

After a while, I noticed that, at times, I was beginning to experience the same symptoms in the restaurant that I had had in the bungalow. Oh, at first I tried to ignore them, thinking it was my imagination. Then I tried to convince myself that this was related to my arthritis. Late in the Fall, when I turned on the furnace in my trailer, I knew it was not my imagination; I was indeed experiencing a severe reaction to gas fumes.

Now I knew that I would have to avoid places where I was exposed to fumes. It was eventually necessary for me to leave the restaurant.

In the time I spent there, I encountered three women who really had a strong influence on the direction my life was to take. The first was Jay, the owner of the restaurant. She was a very caring woman, strong in her faith, well read in scriptures, and aggressive in the cause of Jesus. Through the years, she had taken many under her wing, but, somehow, she always made room for one more. Soon she was sharing her time, her books, and her Lord with me.

The next was Dottie, and she too had a purpose. Dottie knew that I was a convert who had fallen away from the church. Her mission was to take me to a charismatic prayer meeting. Although I refused to go, Dottie continued to call and encourage me to attend.

The next woman I was to meet was Margaret Lynch. She was from St. Aloysius parish, and she had come to the restaurant with a group to enjoy an evening of song. When the evening was over, Margaret approached my table and whispered in my ear, "The Lord has much to give you, if you will only allow him." She then quickly turned and walked away.

As I drove home that evening, I couldn't seem to get this woman out of my mind. How thoughtful of her to share this message with me! It certainly must have taken courage to approach a total stranger, not knowing what my reaction would be. I admired the quality of God's love that I saw in Margaret, and I now wanted to know more about these prayer meetings.

Thrilled with my message and knowing somewhere deep inside that it had truly come from God, I called my friend Dottie. She took me to the Lamb of God prayer group.

The Lamb of God.
My first night at the prayer meeting, January 23, 1986,

was a dramatic experience for me, and certainly one that I shall never forget. The evening started with lots of singing, which captured my heart immediately. Naturally 20 voices joined in song would lift the spirits of anyone.

When the singing ended, they gathered in a circle of prayer, sending their praises to God. In an atmosphere of holiness, I listened intently, trying to grasp the meaning of their prayers. Then there was a time of meditation, while music played softly in the background. When the meditation was over, there was a brief sharing, and then we paired off in twos to pray for one another.

Up until now, I had felt quite satisfied with all of the events that had taken place. Although I did not understand things like the raising of hands and praying in tongues, I still felt fairly comfortable; however praying over someone was definitely a different story. What was I going to do in a situation I knew so little about?

Before I had time to make a decision, I was greeted by a woman named Gloria, who, with a smile, reached out and took my hands. As she began to pray with me, I knew beyond a doubt that this was no stranger. Somewhere in life our paths must have crossed. When my fear began to subside, I entered into her prayers, listening closely as they grew more intense.Soon there were waves of tiny cries coming from deep within her spirit. While she was offering up her petitions for me, I found myself emersed in the light of God's love. Now echoes of joy came bursting forth from the heart of this woman. Then there was a silence between us like the stillness and calm of the night. As we stood together, hand in hand, bound by God's grace, the prodigal in me returned home to the

Father.

Gloria's journey ended that year, for she passed away in the months that followed, her mission of love completed. Like two soul mates on ships that pass in the night, Gloria and I had touched each other's lives, strangers in body, perhaps, but not in spirit. Did I know her? Indeed I did, for deep within dwelled the Christ she had come to share with me.

When I left the prayer meeting that night, I was completely drained of all emotions. Never before had I been through such a powerful experience. Knowing now that a tremendous change had transpired in me, I made the decision to attend the Lamb of God prayer meetings. It took a while before I really felt comfortable praying with others, but the group understood, encouraging me to go at my own pace.*

Within a few weeks Margaret, who had given me God's message in the restaurant, decided that we would meet on a weekly basis for lunch. One of the first things she told me was, if I was willing to be willing, God would change my life. I was willing.

Renew.

Now living back in Bricktown for the winter, I decided to attend St, Martha's prayer group along with my own. This was a very large group, but one filled with love and with a deep commitment for serving Christ. Through St. Martha's I was guided to a family home where I was given an opportunity to enter into *Renew*. This gathering was

---

Charismatic prayer groups, like the Lamb of God, are common to a number of Christian denominations. For the location of one near you, consult your pastor or write Chariscenter USA, P.O. Box 628, Locust Grove, VA 22508-0628.

to awaken both our personal and social growth as active Catholics.

Life in the Spirit.
Three months later the Lamb of God offered me the chance to participate in a "Life in the Spirit" seminar. Charismatic communities give these seminars to prepare persons who are serious about joining them to receive "Baptism of the Spirit". During this ceremony, the community lays hands on and prays over candidates while the candidates renew the personal commitment that they once made to the Lord at baptism. I enrolled in the seminar. It helped me to develop a closer personal relationship with Jesus. Then I was baptized in the Spirit, and committed my life once again to my loving Savior.

The City of Faith
In June some of my Christian friends thought that I should go to the City of Faith, in Tulsa, Oklahoma, for an evaluation of my health.* My prayer group as well as my family helped to finance the trip. Mary, from the Lamb of God, was chosen to accompany me. When we touched down in Tulsa, I was completely moved by the beauty of the countryside.
Mary and I stayed at the Bethany unit in the hospital.

* Catholic Charismatics, as do most other Christians, stress faith and the efficacy of healing prayer. Notwithstanding, they promote concurrent recourse to traditional healing. Humans should not presume to restrict God in the means of His benevolence, and ought to recognize how God commonly chooses to act through the hands (holy hands) of His various servants. Moreover, when God does use miraculous means, expert witnesses from the healing-arts community serve to more acertively proclaim His glory.

This was a wonderful setting to be in, for it was filled with love and prayers. Wherever we went, whether it be to the emergency room or the pharmacy, we were given personal prayers.

Since my tests and consultations were all scheduled during the day time, I was free in the evenings to attend the spiritual activities on the campus. I must tell you that never before had I witnessed so many people in one dwelling. Imagine 5000 Christians of all races and denominations, holding hands and praising the Lord. My seventeen days at the City of Faith was another significant milestone in my spiritual walk.

The Elkins Park Retreat
That November, I attended my first retreat, which was at the Dominican Retreat House in Elkins Park, Pennsylvania. My prayer group had sponsored this retreat. I was quite apprehensive on the day that I arrived, because I didn't really know what to expect., although I was delighted to find that two other members of my prayer group would be rooming with me. Five persons actually shared the room; by the time the first day was over the two who had started out as strangers, were strangers no more.

After dinner that night we gathered for a time of worship and praise. Our Retreat Director, a priest from Utica, New York, opened the conference by asking us to pack up all our cares and worries that we had brought with us, and put them back on the front porch. He said that we had each come seeking God and that this retreat was for us alone. Then, to introduce himself, he shared some of his personal experiences and described his parish ministry. This helped all of us to get better acquainted with him. Feeling comfortable with our director was very important, for many had come bearing personal problems to discuss with him.

In closing, Father gave us a brief message on God's love, and then asked us to return to our rooms in silence and in a spirit of prayer. I was a bit uncomfortable with this, for I had been looking forward to some bedtime laughter, and cheerful conversation Spending time in silence alone with God was something I knew little about. Now, concerned about what I would do if I was unable to sleep, I headed for my room. To my surprise, as I knelt beside my bed that night, God was there to greet me. With much peace I fell off to sleep, looking forward to the next time I could be alone with God.

In the morning there was a 7:30 wake-up call, chapel at eight, and breakfast at nine. By now I was beginning to let my guard down and was starting to feel relaxed and much more enthused about the whole retreat. The day ahead of us was filled with a variety of spiritual activities. There were talks, small group sharings, meditation, walks, prayer time, fellowship and song. The evening with a very moving healing mass. For many this was a time of tears, a time of release, and a time to restore hope to the broken spirit.

The highlight of the retreat was the Holy Eucharist on Sunday. Together, though song and praise, we joined our Lord to become one body. I believe there must have been a spiritual awakening for all, because each seemed to leave with a firm desire to reflect more on God and less on the world. Since then, I have attended several retreats, but none has been as special for me as those sacred moments at Elkins Park.

Inner Healing, and My Call to Ministry

In the spring of 1987 I entered Margaret's Inner Healing Group, and began attending St. Veronica's healing masses celebrated by Father Brendan Williams.

It was then that I began to feel a strong calling for the healing ministry. With little knowledge of what it was all about, I approached my prayer group, asking them to place me on their prayer team. I felt rejected, when at first I didn't get any response; so I continued to pursue the issue. In time, someone explained to me that to discern my readiness for this ministry the group wanted everyone to agree, but they were not yet in agreement. I would just have to wait.

By Fall of that year, recognizing that I truly wanted to serve, the prayer group offered me the music ministry. This humbled me, because I felt that the group members were just trying to pacify me; nevertheless, in an attempt to overcome self, I accepted their offer and soon began a tape ministry for the Lamb of God.

I spent two years fasting and praying, so that the music for each prayer meeting, would correspond with the message and prophecy. Within those two years, by disciplining myself, I developed the art of listening to God.

About two years after I initially petitioned my prayer group to place me on their healing prayer team, they discerned that I was ready. They thus confirmed my original personal discernment that God had called me to this ministry. God's first call was a call of preparation. It prompted me to begin an obstacle-overcoming process of self development that led eventually to the day on which I was actually appointed to the healing ministry.

I have since learned that physical health and emotional stability are desirable prerequisites for serving on such a team. Had I been appointed while still severely wounded in either of these areas, I probably would have had very little to offer to anyone. Praying over people can often be a completely draining experience.

I know today that I needed those years of inner healing sessions, before I could possibly serve on any team. Through God's grace, I realize that our timing is not always his timing, and this must be discerned correctly, if we truly want to do God's will.

Jacob's Well

Another significant episode in my spiritual walk, was my participation in a small study-group called *Jacob's Well*. Inspired by God, a woman named Dottie called together a few of us who were unattached and interested in knowing more about the life of St. Francis.

In the beginning we really weren't sure in what direction the Holy Spirit wanted to lead us. So on Friday nights we gathered for prayer and discernment, followed by the rosary. We used, for our meditations, video tapes about St. Francis, or about the Blessed Mother's reported apparitions at Medugorje.

We continued to meet for several months, seeking God's will, and were then led to become novices in the Secular Order of St. Francis. Dottie was already a member, and, through her encouragement, we began attending monthly meetings at St Cathrine's in Seaside Park.

After three visits of inquiry, we studied as novices for

one year. We learned that the rule of life for the Secular Franciscans is to observe the Gospel of our Lord Jesus Christ, following the examples of St. Francis of Assisi. On June 24, 1990 I was professed. When persons are professed, they are requested to select a new name to symbolize the new life that they will live. The new name is usually the name of a saint whose life has special significance for the candidate. I chose the name, Mary Magdalene.

A Dream Come True.

Since my early twenties, the secret desire of my heart has always been to serve the Lord. It certainly seems odd, that a sinner who felt condemned and unclean,would simultaneously harbor such an impossible dream. Nevertheless Scripture says, "Ask and you shall receive."; through inner healing I learned to ask; through God's grace, I did receive.

During the past five years I have been given many opportunities to evangelize by sharing my testimony, music, and personnel experiences of inner healing. I have witnessed in prayer groups, retreats, workshops and Holy Spirit Seminars. Each commitment has brought with it a time of growth and transformation. Sharing my experience has been a humbling experience, but something I must do for it is my gift to God for all the wonderful things he has done in my life. Today I am a Pastoral leader of the Lamb of God Prayer Community and an active member of their healing team.

Along my path there have been many milestones, each one enriching the quality of my spiritual walk, but none has been so vital as my Inner Healing Group, the place where it all began. Inner Healing was the key that opened the door for Christ's love to transform me. The house on Goldweber Avenue where the Inner Healing sessions were held, was the place where my poor self image was restored to the image and likeness of Christ. What a grace it is that comes to those who are willing to look within! Looking within is certainly not an easy task, but it is one that is well worth the effort, for God's grace opens the heart to love and frees the spirit to live.

Inner healing is a road that leads to God through a journey within the soul. Over the years I have seen the fruits of inner healing in my life and in the lives of others.

Today my soul once surrounded by darkness, lights the path for my spiritual journey. Thank you, God, for a haven of love in a house on Goldweber.

Reflection: The Prodigal Returns
"I'll get up and go to my father and say, 'Father, I have sinned against God and against you,' . . . When [her] father saw [her], he was deeply moved; so he ran and threw his arms around [her]. . . . Later he said, 'This [daughter] of mine was dead, but now [she] is alive; [she] was lost but now I have found [her].' " (This is a paraphrase of Luke 15: 18,20,24 with a change in gender.)

PART TWO

A JOURNEY TO WHOLENESS

After my awakening in the Lamb of God Prayer Community, I used many means to get closer to God. Each of them had a unique value, but for me the most powerful was Inner Healing.

Most chapters in this part, relate to the content of and my reflections on selected Inner Healing sessions, which took place at the home of James and Margaret Lynch, on Goldweber Avenue, in Jackson, New Jersey over a four-year period. The last chapter, however, demonstrates that my special affection for the Blessed Virgin Mary, predates Inner Healing, and even substantially my Catholicism.

Before each meditation contained in these chapters I urge you to pray that the Holy Spirit allow it to have a healing affect in your life as it once did in mine.

HEALING THE ORPHAN

It was in the spring of 1987 at the Lamb of God prayer community in Jackson, New Jersey that I accepted an invitation which changed my life and brought me closer to God. We were invited to Goldweber Avenue, the home of Margaret and James Lynch, to begin an inner healing group. At that time I knew very little about inner healing, but I knew that somewhere deep within my soul was surely dying, and that I must someday begin the long journey back home to the Master.

As the meeting continued, my mind began to wander and my life seemed to flash before me. I remembered that, as a child, I had felt the presence of God within my life, but somewhere between adolescence and maturity the presence of God had faded, the beauty of earth had dwindled and the reason for my existence was no longer known. As the prayer meeting drew to a close, I found myself filled with hope and thrilled with the idea that there was help for me. So I took my new address and went forth in search of my own true identity.

I arrived at 31 Goldweber Avenue with much excitement and anticipation, for I was now convinced that God had a plan for my life. Little did I realize as I walked through that door the struggles of self I would have to encounter, or the pain of growth I would have to endure in order to become the person that God wanted me to be.

As I entered the house I carried with me the scars of years gone by, for my body now reflected the weariness of life itself. As I looked around the room I wondered if anyone would ever understand where I had been in a lifetime.

Our opening sessions were on recognizing our own woundedness. With a room filled with hope, under the guidance of the Holy Spirit, our moderator, Margaret, began to pray diligently for the Holy Spirit to come and fill our hearts with His love. Oh, how I needed to know His love, for the road I had traveled had carried me into the depths of a dying child who needed love in order to survive.

In time and through much prayer and meditation, I began to open like a book with five chapters, each representing an area of woundedness within my life. How frightening this was to find that there was not a part of me that was left without scars.

My mind was in a state of utter emptiness due to the use and abuse of alcohol and drugs. I really no longer knew what Christianity was all about. My heart was recognizable to me only through the pain contained within from the frailty of human love. My physical body, was filled with arthritis; my soul, buried deep in guilt, lay in total darkness. My life was merely an existence waiting upon death.

As we continued to seek the direction of the Holy Spirit, we were led deeper into prayer, and, as we were, a spark of light began to flicker within me. I soon realized that I had received my first healing, for I was now able to recognize the beginning of my own woundedness!

Upon sharing my feelings with the group, I found that exposing my woundedness was a very painful experience, for the sessions were still very new and I had not yet built up a trust among the people. As for our moderator, Margaret, I threw caution to the wind, for my life was hanging by a thread and she was my only hope.

By now the mask that I had worn throughout the years was slowly beginning to dissipate and, like a child whose clothing had been removed, I began to feel naked and totally alone. What was I to do with all this woundedness and how could I ever endure all the pain it brought with it? For as each new hurt began to surface, the pain became more intense. I soon found myself clinging to life and yearning for death at the same time. My body was like a bleeding sore, laid wide open exposing me to all the elements of humanity. Oh, how I yearned for God's eternal medicine! As the blackness of my soul continued to devour me, I cried out in desperation, "My Lord and my God, why hath Thou forsaken me?"

Margaret, in recognizing our utter nakedness and the depths of our sensitivity, now exposed to both ourselves as well as others, quickly but gently led us into an awareness that although we were wounded we were not abandoned. Her teachings were based on scripture, taken first from Isaiah 49:14-15, which confirmed that Jesus did not leave us orphans and we were indeed His children, and second from John 14:16,18, where Jesus said

He would send the Comforter who would abide with us forever.

She explained to us that the feelings we were having of abandonment were not coming from the Father but rather from the "orphan within" who feels deserted and unloved. This little orphan, who is the child within us, rises up from time to time in our lives to let the adult part of us know that we demand attention and healing. When we think negatively it is our orphan. When we feel our family and friends have failed us, it is our orphan.

So many times we look for perfection in others when we ourselves are imperfect. She also explained to us that we desire others to do things the way we perceive to be perfect, but yet we make excuses for ourselves. Our reasons so many times seem to be either " a bad day", "we're not in the mood", or "we just can't be bothered". Yet when others respond to us in this way, we feel hurt and rejected. This is a double standard, the orphan in us expecting perfection from all those people we interact with, yet allowing ourselves to be angry, resentful and imperfect.

As she continued I knew she was talking directly to me, for I was angry, I was resentful and I surely was imperfect. She then interjected that healing is a process and it does not happen overnight. Miracles are immediate, but inner healing takes place gradually over a period of time. She told us our only tool needed now would be a willing spirit to allow God to lead us. We were then brought into meditation and directed to see Jesus as a bridge, a bridge leading us to family and friends, both living and deceased. We called upon the Holy Spirit to reveal the root cause of our search for perfection in others. Afterwards, Margaret instructed us to breathe in the Father's love as we repeated, "Abba loves me, Abba loves me".

Soon I could feel the presence of the Father flowing back into those secret places where I had felt the absence of the Father's love. As the painful memories began to surface, I shared with the Father my sense of His abandonment when people put demands of perfection upon my life. He was there neither to protect me nor to defend me. When I discovered that I was unable to fulfill their demands, I became angry that their expectations of me were set so high, so I in turn came to expect perfection from others. Now clearly came the revelation that the Father had never abandoned me, for it was I who had blocked the Father's love the day I became enslaved to perfection.

As the Father continued to minister to me, I experienced the sensations of both thunder and lightening. Then a beautiful rainbow shown over my life and I knew beyond a shadow of a doubt that God had always held me in the palm of His hand. As this healing was taking place, waves of joy, peace, and freedom began to surge through me; and with it came a sense of belonging that I have never known before. As the group began to share their experience that night, I realized that there was much pain within the room and that their pain was really no different than mine, for we were all God's children and, in some form or another, we were each crying out for His help.

As this session drew to a close, we were blessed with the awareness that recognizing our own "orphan" was a pure gift from God, for only then could we possibly know our need for healing.

Reflection

"... I will not forget you, [my people]. ...I have written your name on the palms of My hands. ... " (Isaiah 49:15,16)

FINDING THE JOY

Before I was introduced to inner healing, I had never given much thought to a "Body of Christ". I suppose if someone had asked me for a description it would have been one filled with love, joy and the sounds of much laughter. I have since learned that happiness is not always the main ingredient, for many times pain and sorrow dwell within a Body; and, unless given the gift of awareness, these traits often go unnoticed.

Most of our inner healing group first met through attending the Lamb of God prayer community. At that time we knew each other in name only, for to truly know someone is to view that person through the eyes of Jesus, and our woundedness prevented us from doing this. To look at us, you would have thought we were happy people. We seemed to have love to give. We wore smiles on our faces and there was laughter heard in our voices but beneath the surface our love was given much reservation, our smiles bore the unseen roots of much pain, and our laughter echoed the sounds of much sorrow. So, although our hands were joined weekly in the same prayer group, our hearts remained strangers to one another. Tell me then, how does a person find the joy that lies within a Body? Is it by weekly attendance in a prayer meeting? For some this is possible, but for others this is most difficult. It is not so easy to find joy praising the Lord when so deeply troubled, nor is it always an easy task to portray the image of a jolly Christian.

As children we're taught that Christians are supposed to be happy people, so we quickly learn to imitate others by putting our best foot forward. As adults we're taught that we should strive to become a reflection of Christ, so others might see that Christ dwells in us. Today I wonder: are the pastures where He dwells a place of peace and serenity, or a place of turmoil and strife? Sometimes in trying so desperately to reflect Christ in our lives, our own true feelings get buried deep within the rubble.

When our group first gathered together we were a broken Body, broken in heart, wounded in spirit. Although we didn't know the depth of our wounds, we each knew in some way that life had taken its toll on us. For life has a way of depriving people of experiencing their own pain, and society tends to discourage them from expressing that pain. I have found that when people are forced to suppress their pain it usually breeds much anger, and eventually this same anger manifests itself in the form of illness, sometimes physical and sometimes emotional.

Why must we always pretend that our feelings do not exist? Wouldn't you like to go some place where you could tell somebody who you really are, and what you really feel? The answer for us was found through inner healing.

I share with you how our group found the joy in the journey of a Body of Christ. It began the same year, the spring of 1987, when some members of our prayer group decided to attend a workshop at Fordham University. This was given by the Lynn brothers and it was on healing our woundedness.

With the exception of Margaret, most of us knew very little about woundedness. It's not that we weren't wounded, but it was a topic that just really never was discussed. Margaret had heard about the workshop and was inspired to go. So through her encouragement, we made the trip with her.

The sessions lasted two days and I think I speak for all of us in saying that it was truly a blessed event. However, to share all our experiences would be impossible, for God touched each soul in a personal way. Throughout the weekend, tears flowed and doors that we didn't know existed were opened for our understanding. Each of us came home with a desire to know the person that we had hidden so well, and although we didn't know it then, this workshop was the beginning of a new life for each of us.

Soon after our return, Margaret announced in our prayer meeting that inner healing was going to begin in her home. Our meetings were held each Tuesday evening with the exception of the third Tuesday of the month, when Father Williams holds his healing mass at St. Veronica's Church in Howell, New Jersey.

We always began each session by praying over one another for God's peace. Some of us felt a little uncomfortable with this at first. Perhaps this was a feeling of unworthiness, or perhaps the fear of change, but nevertheless our feelings were valid and understood. In time, we began to realize the importance of this first step, for when God's peace is prayed over someone the pressures of the day are released. Soon we were each looking forward to our own special time of prayer. When our prayers were finished, we would give glory to God by praising Him in song. In the beginning we sang with little enthusiasm for we were heavily burdened, but graces come to those who try and so we were blessed.

When our singing was over, we would usually sit for a few minutes in silence. Then Margaret would make the sign of the cross and start with an opening prayer, praying always for the guidance of the Holy Spirit to open our path to both the Father and the Son. Each prayer was in preparation for the meditation that was to come. She would then share with us any scripture she had been given throughout the week and lead us into the meditation.

In the beginning the meditations were somewhat difficult, for letting go of self is not something we could do overnight, especially when we had spent a lifetime building up walls of resistance. Now all of a sudden we were being asked to give up control, to surrender our rebellious nature and to seek discipline within our lives. To master this seems like it would surely take forever, but Margaret quickly assured us that living one day at a time would bring the best results; for wanting tomorrow yesterday robs us of appreciating our own spiritual walk. As Margaret showered us with patience and understanding, our impulsiveness soon subsided. In time the meditations became a welcomed blessing for they gave us the freedom to journey inward, and so our lives began to change.

Each meditation brought new insights, giving us a desire to express ourselves and a willingness to be open with one another. It wasn't long before we realized that being ourselves was not impossible, for it was our God-given right. We soon discovered that tears were accepted in exchange for smiles, and anger when directed by love was encouraged for the good of our general health. Now we were beginning to trust one another so there was little hesitation in our honesty. We talked with confidence for we knew we were treating each other the way we ourselves wanted to be treated. Our confidence allowed us the freedom to express our shortcomings, for we found no judge nor juror among us.

At the close of each meditation there would be a time for sharing if we so desired. I believe this is how our little Body began to grow in wholeness, the day we took our eyes off self and put them on each other. Oh naturally this didn't happen overnight, for we were all in need of love, but the day did come when we no longer needed to be the center of attention. We found ourselves willing to give our prayers and support to the one who needed it most; for meditation could be very painful experiences, especially when walking back through those memories that we had either buried or forgotten. These were trying times for all of us, , so we welcomed the support that was given by our sisters and brothers. With compassion we listened as one by one we shared our pain. As the tears began to flow, I realized that we were being bathed in love by the very tears that fell from one another. With each new experience we have reinforced in each other the precious gift of self worth, allowing us to discover our own inner beauty.

In closing we always joined in a circle of prayer, giving

thanks to God for all the healings that had taken place during the evening. We would then say the "Our Father", the "Hail Mary" and the "Glory Be".

As I look back over the past four years, I see many wonderous revelations. Can you imagine the beauty of being healed by nursing the wounds of one another? God has truly manifested Himself in our brokenness. Guided by the light of the Holy Spirit we have walked through the desert of darkness, passing from death of self to the resurrection of new life. We have learned the meaning of loving, both in sickness and in health. We have learned the true value of living is found in the giving, rather than in the receiving. We have learned that God's grace gives us the freedom to explore the depths of our own spirituality. In the stillness of those nights, we have found the reflection of Jesus in one another. We know today that Jesus lies beneath the pain of every living creature.

So, until you have dried each other's tears, dressed each other's wounds, shouldered each other's cross and walked a mile in each other's shoes, only then will you find the true joy that swells within the Body of Christ.

Reflection
"So then, confess your sins to one another and pray for one another, so that you will be healed." (James 5:16)

FAMILY TREE

In John 4 we find the Bible passage of the woman at the well and Jesus says, "The hour is already here when true worshipers will worship the Father in Spirit and Truth". This is the kind of worship the Father wants. God is Spirit and those who worship must worship in Spirit and Truth; and because we are made in His image and likeness, we are also Spirit. So we can see how important it is to the Father to have our spirits freed.

When God first touched us we were very brittle; there was a hard shell around us. We weren't malleable to His touch; we really weren't ready to be softened, but now we are.

Margaret's Meditation
So tonight we pray that the Spirit will guide us into the fullness of the Father's embrace, so that our spirits can experience the fullness of His grace.

Begin now by feeling the warmth of His love and the strength of His arms wrapped around you. As He embraces you, you tune into the sound of His heartbeat. You find your own heartbeat beginning to pick up speed as you join in with the strong, powerful rhythm of the Father's. The Father shifts position from time to time, but you remain in His embrace.

In the stillness of the night you wait for the Father to speak. He then tells you that He is going to take you to the podium where Jesus will be waiting for you. You feel very secure as you walk with the Father in the direction of Jesus. As you round the bend you see Jesus, and you know immediately that He is the Jesus of Mercy that has come for you. As you stand before Him in the glow of all His radiance, He extends His hand to you. With trust you put your hand in His because you know that He has died for you. As you step up to the podium Jesus says, "It is now time to look at your own family tree".

You notice that there is a book in front of you, a very beautiful book, and on its cover is written your name and your birthdate. Jesus places your hand upon the cover and you open the book to the first page labeled

The Royal Family". At the top of the page you see the name "God the Father", and Jesus invites you to see Him as your true father. The next name is "Jesus, Lord and Saviour, son of God and Jesus your brother". You now see the name written "Holy Spirit", the One who is your advocate and your friend. As you look further you see the name "Mary, mother of God and Mary, your mother", and "Joseph, foster father of Jesus and your foster father". You begin to see the names of the saints now. You see Matthew, Mark, Luke and John. You see Thomas, the doubting one; you see Peter and all the saints who mean so much to you. You belong to a long line of saints. It is part of your heritage, for you are a member of the family of God.

Mary comes. She asks you to turn the page of the book, for she wants to see your family. So with the Lord's help you say "yes", and you turn the page. There, you see your own family tree. You see all the blessings that God has poured out upon your family, a family chosen by God just for you.

My Healing

As I began to examine my family tree, I saw the richness of God's love fall upon the spirit of each family member. One by one, I watched their beauty unfold. I wondered why I had never seen this beauty before. I soon realized, for the first time in my life, I was viewing them through the eyes of Jesus, rather than with the human eye. As I watched with awe of what was taking place, my mind flashed back to the cover of the book, and once again I saw my date of birth. I wondered why it appeared to be so large, for it seemed to be larger in size than the print of my own name.

As I thought about this, I was taken to Bethlehem to the place of the Nativity, When I entered the stable, Joseph, Mary and baby Jesus appeared before me. I watched with delight as they showered their love upon Jesus. Soon the scene began to change and Mary was no longer recognizable as Mary. Another woman was there now and, although she looked familiar to me, I couldn't quite place who she was. I decided to move in closer, hoping to get a better look at her.

As I neared the circle my tears began to flow, for the woman I was looking at was my own mother. I looked further now and I found my father to be kneeling where Joseph had once knelt. With hope in my heart I quickly dropped my eyes hoping to get a glimpse of Jesus, but much to my surprise, the child within the manger was the image of myself.

Startled, I jumped back disbelieving what I had just seen.

Then I heard the voice of the Father saying, "Look beyond your humanness and see the holiness of your own family". As I listened to the Father's words, I realized that I had never once thought of my family as a holy family, nor had I ever thought of their heritage as being of God.

As Margaret played the closing song, new revelations began to surface within me. In those joyful moments I realized that my family tree was now bringing new meaning to me. The nativity of Jesus, Mary and Joseph was a sign to show me that God had created each member of my family in holiness. He had joined us in love so that we could become a family unit and live the Gospel together. My birthdate on the cover was outstanding to me so that I might know that my birth was just as meaningful to God as was Jesus' birth. I was placed in His crib so I might see my own importance.

Today I know that each member of my family is a branch of God's body, and our bond of unity forms the tree that once led to Calvary. As for me, I now know that I am a special part of that tree, special to God and special to my family.

Group Sharing

Some people, due to bitterness and rejection within their own families, found it comforting for a while to become the child of the Royal Family. In closing the session, we each felt that we were an active part of Christ's body.

Reflection

"Christ is like a single body, which has many parts; it is still one body, even though it is made up of different parts. In the same way, all of us . . . have been baptized into the one body by the same Spirit, and we all have been given the one Spirit to drink." (1 Corinthians 12,13)

PART TWO: CHAPTER FOUR

FORGIVING OUR PARENTS

How often in life have we expected our parents' forgiveness, yet have been unwilling to forgive them for their mistakes! As children we learn to take forgiveness for granted, for it is just something that a parent does. It seems to come with the job of being a good parent. But when the roles are reversed, and we are the ones expected to do the forgiving, we find it to be an almost impossible task.

It's hard to imagine that we grow up believing that we should always be on the receiving end of forgiveness. How sad is this misconception, for while deceiving ourselves, we deprive our parents of their own true gift of humanness. As adults we seem to lose sight of the fact that our parents were once children too, and, just as we have felt hurt, neglected, misunderstood, and at times verbally abused, they too at some point in their youth must have felt exactly the same way. I believe that in order to understand the responses that were given to us we must first seek out the childhood of the child who parented us.

I realize today that as much as I loved my grandparents, I never knew them as parents. For I was their granddaughter and their response to me was always one of love. I really do not know in what manner they raised their own children, but I think for most of us who are still searching for answers within the realm of our own childhood reality, we must someday look beneath the rubble within the lives of our own parents.

What were their lives really like, and what can we learn from their past that might help us in coping with ours? Was their home one filled with love and were they given much affection? Were both parents living in the home? Was there discipline and, if so, was it given with compassion or was it physical abuse? Were they under stress due to financial difficulties? Was there alcohol within the home? Was there sickness within the family? Was your mother or father an only child or were there several children, making it highly impossible to receive the attention they needed? Were they the oldest and were they responsible for all the others? These are just some of the questions we must find the answers to, for only when we are able to see their woundedness will we be able to understand our own.

As I view humanity today through the eyes of an adult, I can see that no one is perfect, not even parents, and why should they be; we are not. They are entitled to make mistakes just as we are. And tell me, why should they always be expected to act like adults; we don't. If at times there's a child in us, then there's bound to be one in them. Why is it when things get rough we allow our child to surface, and yet we expect theirs to remain hidden? And oh how often have we been quick to judge their motives and slow to praise their efforts.

Perhaps it is time to reevaluate our families. Jesus says to forgive seventy times seven. So tell me, have you forgiven your parents for their mistakes, or are you still harboring resentments? The scriptures clearly state that what we bind on earth will be bound in heaven. Isn't it about time that we released our parents from the bondage we've held them in? Scripture also states that we all have fallen short of the glory of God. So who are we to refuse forgiveness to one another? It matters not whether your family is living or deceased. For God grants miracles in Heaven as surely as He does on earth. Today I ask you to open up your hearts and allow your parents the joy of being free. The day will come when you will no longer need to be always right, for with forgiveness comes maturity as well as many blessings. For only when you can say, "I forgive" will you become the person that you desire to become. Remember, if you are made in the image and likeness of Christ, so is the unforgiven parent.

Reflection

". . . Be kind and tender hearted to one another, and forgive one another, as God has forgiven you through Christ." (Ephesians 4:32)

BITTER ROOTS

We have the main responsibility to make sure that there are no bitter roots from our childhood springing up, regardless of whatever anyone says or does to us. As spirit-filled Christians, we are responsible for this. Whatever judgements we made as children carry over into our present relationships with others right now. It is a cycle. What we sow is what we reap. In the law of God everything multiplies. So if we sow a small bitter seed it multiples. It continues to grow; it increases in size and in strength. This is a spiritual law, an important thing to be aware of. Just as all of God's blessings have multiplied, so do the feelings that aren't blessings to us, and most of them stem from childhood.

For example, if a father didn't walk, feed and give care to child, a part of that child's spirit wasn't nurtured as it should be. If you didn't get the touch and love that you needed, then there is a part of your spirit that withdrew, and in the withdrawing it sowed a bitter seed. If a father deprives a child of this attention, the child will most likely grow up with some kind of emotional problems. We all need the attention of both father and mother because God created us this way.

If someone in your life hurts you and you say, "I'll never let anyone hurt me again", you are sowing a bitter root. The law of judgement causes you to be powerless because you have judged others. If a father wasn't there for you, then you will not trust other men; you will put up a wall between you and men. This is your expectancy that comes from your bitter root. So with all men you will hold back a part of yourself. This is the cycle that goes on and, as it does, you have made a judgement that you don't trust men. It is how you perceive things from the past, not necessarily how they really were. You must break the power of this cycle.

It's hard for everyone to let go because of past woundedness, and because we expect to be disappointed by people, we try to control. It is just a reaping of what we have sown. I don't think anyone is exempt or excluded from this law. So tonight we are going to pray to release these bitter roots.

Margaret's Meditation
Lord, we ask You to send Your Spirit to help us to make this journey. We ask the Holy Spirit to help us make that conscious decision as an adult to forgive and to be forgiven. Whatever we find at the depths of our being, we ask the Lord that You would shine Your light and give us the guidance as we go to meet the wounded child within. Lord, put out Your hand to give us the courage we need. Lord, we need Your help, Your light and Your love. Because of bitter roots we're fearful to meet You Lord.

We're fearful of meeting the child within us, but we enter a place of light, a warm glowing light, a really peaceful atmosphere, Lord.

We see You sitting in the chair, Lord, and we see ourselves sitting on Your lap. We're little, Lord, and we reach up to touch Your face and stroke your beard. Lord, You have Your arms around us. We feel the security of that male touch and the strength of Your arms around us. You are so gentle, Lord, as You wipe the tears from our cheeks. We didn't expect that from a male. There is no time, Lord; You have so much time just to hold us and let Your love flow through us. We ask, Lord, why are we fearful. The Lord answers, "Fear not being loveable and being loved". We fear our fathers going away; we fear being left alone. You, Lord, tell us not to fear, to trust in You, that You will take care of us.

And, Lord, when You ask us to hand You our bitter roots against our fathers, You give us the grace to forgive our fathers for whatever they did not do to meet our needs. So we are able to hand You those bitter roots. There is a charcoal fire near You, Lord, and as we hand them to You, You throw those bitter roots upon the fire. The sparks and flames shoot up and the roots burn. Into our empty hands, Lord, You put gifts of joy, peace and love, gifts of freedom that we didn't have before. We feel the warmth of Your fire, Lord, and we feel comforted and loved. We thank You, Lord, for freeing this child within us. We no longer feel bound, Lord, and we thank you for breaking the chains of bondage. We thank You for Your unfailing and unending love.

My Healing

This meditation brought with it a desire to know more about my past. I now wondered just how many bitter roots I had sown within my family. I wondered if I had left home carrying a suitcase full, and if so were there any bearing my father's name. I was very fortunate to have a loving father and, although his role in my life was different than most fathers, he still seemed to meet my needs. Many people think of a father as the one who has the aggressive personality, the one who becomes the authority figure, and above all the one who supports the family, My father was the bread winner but his personality was not aggressive, nor was he the authority figure within our household.

During this meditation I could think of no earthly reason why I would ever sow a bitter root against my father, for he was my father and to me he could do no wrong. Oh perhaps I didn't always get the touch that I needed when I thought I needed it, and perhaps at times he wasn't attentive to my needs; and it's true he didn't always defend me when I thought he should have, and perhaps I would have liked it more if once in a while he would have yelled at me, if only for the sake of his attention.

As I continued to meditate, I realized I had deluded myself into believing that my dad was always perfect; and now I found myself making excuses for his human imperfections. As I began to glance back over my past, I was able to recognize the bitter roots that I had sown so many years ago. In that moment I realized that my dad was a man prone to mistakes just like everyone else, and while looking at his imperfections I was able to see that he had met my needs to the best of his ability.

I now had a desire to surrender each of my bitter roots, so I reentered the scene of the meditation. As I neared the fire once again I could see that Jesus was waiting for my return. One by one, I handed Him my bitter roots and He lowered them into the fire. As together we watched them burn, I somehow knew they were gone forever.

Group Sharing

For some, this meditation was rather difficult, for it was not easy releasing our bitter roots. Some were fearful of letting go while others were more trusting. As the Lord blessed us with new insights that evening, we were each better able to understand that harboring bitter roots only hinders our spiritual journey.

Reflection

"See to it that no one be deprived from the grace of God and that no bitter root spring up and cause trouble through which many may be defiled" (Hebrews 12:15, *The New American Bible with Revised New Testament.* Nashville: Thomas Nelson, 1987.)

WE ARE SPECIAL

Have you ever thought of how special you are, and how unique you are in the sight of God? Many people feel that when they were born they weren't really wanted or loved. So they spend most of their lives looking for reasons why they shouldn't have been born. They tend to accumulate over the course of years all the negative things that people have said and done to them. These negative feelings, when added up, seem to reinforce their own beliefs. Eventually these same feelings rob them of any self worth they might have had, leaving them with a very poor self image.

Once they have convinced themselves they are worthless, they develop a habit of putting themselves down before anyone else gets a chance. So they spend their lives grieving their birth and dwelling on the negatives rather than focusing on all the positives. Oh, how much of life they really miss. It is not important whether or not you think your parents wanted you at the time of your conception, or whether the circumstances were good or bad. The important thing is that God wanted you to be conceived, to be born and to be living here and now. You are the wonderous work of God. You have been created in His image and likeness and you are His very own child.

Margaret's Meditation

Tonight the Father wants you to see yourself as truly a creation of His love. So we are going to have a time of healing of the time of your conception. We journey back now to the beginning of your life. It is the day before your conception and you can hear the Father speaking softly as He tells you, "before I formed you in the womb I knew you". Picture in your mind the throne room of Heaven. God the Father is in the throne room. The Father now begins to survey the earth. He looks down and sees your parents and He sees their home. He decides that what is most needed for them is for a child to be born. So the Father decided to create you. He has a picture of you in His heart, and because He is all love He creates you in pure love.

He now looks down upon your parents and He says, "It is time". The Father knew exactly what you were going to need so He picked your parents for you because of their specific characteristics, and He chose you to bring His love to them. Try to sense in your spirit the love of the Father. The world tries to crush this love but it cannot because you are so special in His eyes.

Remembering that the Father has been with you since before your birth, you begin now to feel His loving Presence as you enter into the womb of your mother. Allow yourself to feel the warmth and love of your mother. Feel her heartbeat and her nourishment for you.

Feel the gentleness of her embrace flowing into you. Be assured by her tenderness that you are in a place that is safe and secure. Stretch out your tiny but perfect little body and feel the freedom as your spirit picks up the tranquility and peacefulness. It is a time for growing and developing for you are free from all anxiety and tensions. You find your surroundings to be an atmosphere of contentment. As you bask in the love of your mother's womb you now let go of any negative feelings of unwantedness. You begin to sense a tremendous love as you feel the joy of being welcomed by your parents upon this earth.

[As this session drew to a close, we each rested in the womb for a long time.]

My Healing

During the meditation I had a vision of a beautiful sunset, and the Father stood just beyond. In the midst of the clouds, He took a deep breath and He breathed life into the womb of my mother. My healing was found in the sunset for it showed me the beauty of my own creation.

Group Sharing

Through sharing our experiences we seemed to draw each other closer to knowing that it was truly the Father's will that brought us into this world and that our parents were chosen of God. Margaret's meditation made us realize that there is a specialness in God's works and we must enter into it and take the grace from it. For we are the creation of His love and the wonder of His works. So often in our feelings of unworthiness we fail to see God's gift to us, which is the miracle of ourselves.

Reflection

"When my bones were being formed, carefully put together in my mother's womb, when I was growing there in secret, you knew I was there— you saw me before I was born. . . . " (Psalm 139:15,16)

ARE YOU LOOKING FOR JESUS?

When Jesus spoke to Mary Magdalene she did not recognize Him as Jesus until He called her by name. Mary, thinking He was the gardener, said, "Sir, if you have taken Him away, tell me where you have put Him and I will go and remove Him." Only when Jesus said the name "Mary" did she recognize Him as Saviour. She then called out to Him using the name "Rabboni" which means Master.

Lots of times Jesus speaks to us but we neither hear nor see Him until He calls us by name. I think most of us can identify with Mary Magdalene. We each find areas of sinfulness in our lives, and then we hear Jesus call us by name. He calls us out of sinfulness and into new life.

Margaret's Meditation
Let's begin tonight by taking a couple of deep breaths, and breathe out anything that is bothering you from today, so that you can really hear the Lord when He calls you by name.

You are at the tomb of Jesus, early in the morning; it's still dark. Feel the dew of the grass on your feet as you walk in search of Jesus. You can see the stars as they begin to fade from the sky. Darkness gives way to morning and daylight begins to shine forth. You find yourselves feeling anxious for you don't know if you are going to be able to find Jesus, or if the stone at the tomb will keep you separated from Jesus. You don't even know if anyone will be there to help you roll away the stone. As you hurry through the garden you look for someone who will help you with the stone.

As you approach the tomb, you stop suddenly because you can see that the stone has already been rolled away. Then you see two men running toward the tomb. As they enter the tomb you watch with great expectations, for you're hoping to get a glimpse of Jesus. Soon they return but, much to your disappointment, without Jesus. You hesitate for a few minutes and then you enter the tomb looking for Jesus. You see the angels with a radiance and glow that shines all around them. They ask you why you are there and you say, "I've come to find the One who died for me; I come to find Jesus". The angels say, "Why do you look for Him here; He is gone". So you turn to leave and, as you do, there is a gardener standing there; He asks you why you are leaving.

Go back to the scene in the garden now and picture yourself as Mary Magdalene. You and Mary are one, and the reason you are looking so intently for Jesus is because He has loved you so much. You were a sinner but He never accused you. He just forgave you and He loved you totally, just exactly as you were. So you gave your heart to Him as you never gave to anyone else. It's a total love relationship between you and Jesus. Now you deeply feel the absence of His love. You have seen Him abused, beaten, scorned. You saw Him drag Himself through the streets with the cross on His shoulders, and you felt the agony of love in your heart for Him as you saw Him die. You heard Him as He cried out to the Father, "Forgive then for they know not what they do". These words were a security to you, for you knew what it was to be forgiven much. So with all your heart you wanted to find Jesus again.

Now you are leaving the tomb and you meet the gardener. Listen for the voice of Jesus as He calls you by name. Do you recognize the voice as Jesus' voice? Do you believe that He is calling you? Do you accept the love that He gives freely through the act of His calling? Do you open your self totally to Him, or are you afraid to trust the love in His voice? Are you looking for proof that it is really Jesus? Are you searching for the wound marks in His hands and the thorn marks on His forehead, or can you believe just by the sound of His voice that it is truly Jesus. The Jesus who was crucified, died and rose again has come back. He is now waiting for you in His garden.

[The meditation ended with the song, "Just Like You Promised, You Would Come".]

My Healing
My healing was in recognizing my own inattentiveness to Jesus' call. I wondered then just how many times I have been the unlistening servant and have refused to respond to His call. I, like Mary Magdalene, was still looking for the "Human Jesus". Peter and John, upon entering the tomb, found it empty and so believed in the resurrected

Christ. Mary and I had not yet reached that spiritual plane. Now all of a sudden while in the garden, I was able to recognize the resurrected Jesus, and I could hear His call as He so clearly said, "Your garden is within, Pam, come follow me."

Group Sharing
In our group that night Margaret's thought was that we must each allow ourselves to go through the Magdalenes in order to appreciate Jesus and also to experience the gift of forgiving love.

Reflection
"Then she turned around and saw Jesus standing there; but she did not know it was Jesus.... She thought He was the gardener, . . ." (John 20:14, 15)

HAVE YOU BROKEN FELLOWSHIP WITH GOD?

Most of us don't really know or understand the Father's love because our ideas of love have been shaped by our families, our relatives or our childhood friends. It therefore is a slanted view because no matter how perfect or imperfect our families were, there is no possible way that their love could be anything like the Father's love for us. In our busy world we should take time daily to meditate upon the Father's love, for it is truly a resource for us.

When God created man, He created him in the image of Himself. Male and female, God really created us to meet Him face to face. When God created the Garden and Adam and Eve, He created it so they could be in communion with Him. God wanted to be present to them and to share all of creation with man. Adam and Eve knew they had fallen whey they ate the fruit. They knew they had broken fellowship with God and so they tried to hide themselves.

Margaret's Meditation

When we were created we each fellowshiped with God, but at some point in time we were tempted and we fell. Tonight as we enter into prayer we are going to ask God to reveal to us that specific time in our lives when we broke fellowship with Him.

Picture yourself in the Garden with beautiful flowers all around you. Sense the beauty that this Garden holds. Hear the birds as they sing with much joy. There is a great light shining as the sun begins to set. Now twilight time falls upon the earth. Soon you begin in hear familiar sounds of God, the Father's footsteps coming toward you. Your impulse is to go and hide because you are afraid to meet the Father, for you know that He is aware that you have broken that link of fellowship between you.

As the Father begins to search for you, He calls you to come into His presence. You hesitate because you don't want the Father to judge you. You wait for a moment and then you begin to move in His direction. As you stand before Him, He opens both arms wide and He waits to receive you. [Our meditation ended with the song. "Only a Shadow of Your Love for Me".]

My Healing

I was unable to go to the Father in this meditation. I found myself standing as an adult behind a tree with a black mask on. I was naked and my nakedness represented my sin. My healing came in recognizing that it was I who had broken fellowship with God the day I allowed sin to enter my life.

Group Sharing

Some were able to come out to meet the Father while others were not. Some saw the Father looking at them through the eyes of love, and others were hesitant to trust in His love. Nevertheless, by the end of the evening each of us had come to a better understanding that we ourselves had broken the chain between God and man.

Reflection

"Your conduct was perfect from the day you were created until you began to do evil." (Ezekiel 28:15)

TO KNOW JESUS AS SAVIOUR

God is calling us as Christians to be His light. There is darkness all around us, in our homes and with our friends. It is very important for us to join in prayer, to unite and to share with one another our love of Him. Together we must grow and be strengthened in that love. We must become light and share His love with the world.

Margaret's Meditation

Tonight God wants us to know Him as Saviour so we can be His light. In Luke it says, "today in the town of David a Saviour has been born to you". The angel did not say he had been born to Mary or Joseph, The angel said that he had been "born to you". It is so important to know that for each of us a Saviour has been born.

The shepherds knew that this was the Saviour that the angel had told them about because they followed the Light which led them to Him. In the same way, God is calling us to know Him as Saviour. Ninety percent of the time we seem to know that He is our Saviour, but the other ten percent we are never quite sure. Like the shepherds,we must have no doubt in our minds, so that to whomever we meet we can testify to what we know to be true. The only way our witness is any good is when it is without a shadow of a doubt.

A saviour is one who frees us from the past. This means freeing us from any past sins, any past bad habits, past pains and past hurts, whatever is wounding us and binding us to the past. Jesus wants to heal and free us from it. Go now with the Holy Spirit and let the Lord show you those moments that were most painful in your life.

In the stable when Jesus was born, there was a glow of warmth and love. The Lord would want you to open yourself to that same love, so that glow, that light, can shine on your woundedness and you can be healed. The Lord is coming tonight as a healing Saviour, to heal the pains of Christmases Past. So let the light of love shine through as the Holy Spirit reveals to you the reality of your pain. Now let us reflect on Mary and Joseph's journey to the first Christmas. Imagine the painful sacrifice that Mary made by going on that journey. How tiring and uncomfortable it must have been to be pregnant and riding on a donkey. Joseph also made a sacrifice when he was told by the angel to go, and so in obedience he went. He too must have endured the pains of concern, not knowing how long the journey would take or where they might find shelter.

At the birth of the Saviour, the first Christmas, Mary and Joseph were healed of the pain of their past journey. We too, as we come to know Jesus as Saviour, are healed of the pain of Christmases Past. Our mission here on earth is to follow that star, the light of the first Christmas; for to know Jesus as Saviour we must first make that long painful journey.

My Healing

As I listened to the message, I was able to make the journey with Mary and Joseph. As I crossed the miles I began to reflect on the only painful Christmas I can ever remember. It was Christmas morning and my brother was Santa Claus. As he passed out the presents one by one, I patiently waited for my gifts. I received many that day, but the one I was waiting for was not among my presents. When my sister opened her gifts and I realized that she had received the present that I wanted, I was devastated. As I sat beside the tree the tears began to well up within me. I don't know how I contained all the pain I felt at that moment. I was crushed to think that my parents would deliberately hurt me like that. As I tried to hide my tears I wandered off into my bedroom. Much later in the morning they found me in tears. As soon as they realized what had happened, they searched for my other gift. Sure enough, it was found beneath the back of the tree. Although the problem was resolved, I can still feel the pain of the disappointment in that little child.

Today as I surrender that pain, the adult within me recognizes all the beautiful Christmases I've had, and just how blessed my life has really been. As the meditation drew to a close I realized the past no longer mattered, for my eyes were fixed on Jesus, the Saviour who had come for me. Through this message I have learned that my life can become a fulfillment of the Saviour's promises.

Group Sharing

As the group began to share, much pain began to surface. One experience was of a child who was found peeking at a present much before Christmas. When Christmas morning arrived, she found all her presents to be unwrapped, Another was a similar experience but the child found only one present to be under the tree, the one that she had opened before Christmas.

As our sharing came to a close, we were each better able to focus upon the Christmas journey and what it means in our individual lives. We realized that to truly know Jesus takes a lifetime, but to find Him only takes today. The joy found in this message is in knowing that as we come to know Jesus day by day, we can share that light along the way.

Reflection

The Word was the source of life, and this life brought light to mankind. The light shines in the darkness, and the darkness has never put it out." (John 1:4,5)

EXPECTATIONS OF OTHERS

Are you the person who God created you to be or are you just trying to live up to the expectations of others? An example of this is a man who spent his life putting himself in a position of trying to be someone who he really wasn't. He was always trying to do the "right thing", what other people thought he should do. I don't really think he ever stopped to ask them, so it was his own expectations of what he thought other people wanted. Nevertheless, he was constantly putting demands upon himself. Through the strain of trying to be a perfect father, a perfect husband and a perfect employee, he became an alcoholic. Through prayer he was freed of his alcoholism, but he was never freed of his alcoholic personality. He was always striving to be perfect, and naturally none of us are. In trying so hard to please everyone he never learned how to give up control, so God's healing love could free him. He wouldn't let himself to be the person God created him to be.

I find that I need to I take time out for myself to

become myself. Only when I free myself from the demands of being a worker, a mother, a wife, a friend, can I become the person who God created me to be. We each of us need to take time out for ourselves. Instead of trying be trying to fill a void within us, allow God to fill it as it should be filled.

We have now come to the time when God wants to move us to where He wants us to be. He wants us to stand on Holy Ground, to come before Him, stripped of all those expectations that were never His. In Jeremiah, He tells us that He knew us before we were born, so He knew just what He wanted each one of us to be. Tonight let us come to Him, stripped of everybody else's expectations.

Margaret's Meditation
Father, we ask for the gift of willingness to give up our rebellious nature and to surrender whatever woundedness keeps us from being what You want us to be. We know that You are our Abba, our loving Father, and only when we accept your love can we be freed. We ask You to help us accept our own imperfections, knowing that we don't have to be perfect in anything; we just have to be free to do the things that You want us to do.

When You created us, You had specific jobs for us, but we have taken on all these other jobs that the world expects of us. Through our own free will we have made these choices and we have accepted these roles. Father, we come before You now; we seek your love and we ask You to free us from the expectations of others and from the roles that we have assumed throughout our lives.

(During the silence of our group meditation, our sister Lynn was inspired by the Holy Spirit to reveal to each of us the nursery rhyme character that we had patterned our lives after. Margaret then reminded us of Heidi's story and how, when she was taken from the Swiss Alps to the city, her spirit became stifled.)

Most of us seem to be in a position where our spirits are stifled, and God wants to release us so we can be the persons we were created to be. So let's go back into visualizing ourselves as the nursery rhyme characters that the Holy Spirit revealed. Remember, the Father wants us to be set free from these characters and transform us into His perfect creation.

We come now before Abba. Our feet are bare; we are standing on Holy Ground. Abba's loving presence surround us. He welcomes us with open arms. We take time now to let the peace of the Father's Spirit enter into ours. We begin to sense our own spirits struggling to be freed from our nursery rhyme characters. We tell the Father that we are willing to move on from the place where we are bound to the place of freedom that He has for us. In this moment of Grace, by the power of His son Jesus, we are transformed and freed of our worldly expectations.

My Healing
This meditation was the beginning of many small miracles for me, for I realized that in all my life I had never once been the person who God had created me to be. Never once had I trusted God enough to show me who I really was. Through my own insecurities I had tried to live my life by reflecting the personalities of those around me. In doing so, I placed many demands upon myself. As others saw me in various roles, they too placed demands upon me which I found impossible to meet. Through the strain

of it all, I grew further and further away from myself.

The day came when I no longer wanted responsibility, for coping with responsibility represented maturity, and maturity meant surrendering my childhood. Before long I found I was caught up in a world of make-believe. As I grew older, my desires became few, for I now had only two: one was to please people so they would like me; the other was to stay young so they would love me.

As this session drew to a close the Holy Spirit tapped upon my shoulder once again, reminding me that I must live my life in the truth of who I really am. That night I surrendered to God my fantasy figure of Peter Pan, the child who never grew up. I left there with a gift of new hope, hope of finding and expressing my own personality, hope of experiencing my new-found freedom.

Only when there is hope in our hearts can we grow into the persons God created us to be.

Group Sharing
This night freedom brought the release of many tears. One by one we silently bid farewell to— Wendy, Little BoPeep, Heidi, Jack, Jill, Peter Pan, Pinocchio, the China doll, and the lion in the Wizard of Oz. We found that we no longer needed to live disguised. We were now set free to live our lives according to God's plan and to fulfill only His expectations.

Reflection
"Freedom is what we have— Christ has set us free! Stand then as free people, and do not allow yourselves to become slaves again." (Galatians 5:1)

LAMB OF GOD

Do you still believe that God is a punishing God, or do you know Him as a loving Father? When we are baptized in the Holy Spirit, our relationship with God the Father should begin to change. As we grow closer to Him each day, we should begin to see Him as a loving God, not punishing but just. We must always remember that God proved how great His love was for us when He sent His only Son into this world so that our sins might be forgiven. Through Jesus' death, we have been washed clean by the Blood of the Lamb.

We as Christians, coming into new life through baptism, have a responsibility to grow and to change. If we are adults then we have a responsibility to come to Jesus as adults. We come to the Father as children, but we are supposed to come to Jesus as adults. This is our call to holiness. If we spend our whole lives coming to Jesus as children, then there is something wrong with our walk to holiness. There is naturally a period of time when we do come to Jesus as children in the beginning of our relationship, but then Scripture tells us that we must stop having the milk and start eating solid food. So at some point we are supposed to come as adult to adult, knowing that we are forgiven by Jesus.

So many times when something is triggered off within us our memory takes us back to childhood, and we relate once again as a child to a fearful God. In our lives we must always be aware that the enemy is at work, trying to convince us that God is judging us. Sometimes we find this is caused from guilt and sometimes fear, but whatever the reason we should always stop and experience an inner healing process upon ourselves.

We should start by bringing Jesus into the situation and asking Him to take us to the Father. We go to the Father as a child, so we come with that childlike trust and confidence. The Father sees us through the eyes of Jesus, so He sees us pure and spotless. Isn't it comforting as Christians to know that we don't have to walk through anything alone anymore? All we have to do is call on Jesus and He will take us to the Father.

Margaret's Meditation
We are going to come into prayer tonight and we are going to picture Jesus, the Lamb of God, with us. We are thankful that You are our Lord and Redeemer, that You are the crucified Lord. We know it is by Your cross that we are set free and by Your stripes we are healed. We now bring that part of ourselves that has been bruised and wounded, the part that feels guilty, soiled and dirty. We bring that to You, Lord Jesus, to be touched, to be cleansed, to be washed, free from stain, to be healed. We ask You to make us new by Your healing touch and by the

Blood of the Lamb.

We come to You, Lord, in Your pasture, and we come as Your sheep. Some of us , Lord, are just a little off-white; some feel gray and some feel black, but through Your eyes, Lord, we know that we are all shining white. So we come as we are. We come in a line, one by one. We wait patiently upon one another for our turn to come before You.

We watch as You lift the little gray lamb in Your arms; we listen to Your whispers telling him of Your love and forgiveness. We watch, Lord Jesus, as Your touch comes upon him and the grayness fades away. Soon Your radiance begins to shine forth over the little lamb. Now You put him over Your shoulders and that healed lamb starts to pray for the next lamb. This one, Lord, is a lamb that feels it is black, so You pick it up and You hold it close to You. As your hearts beat together, the lamb begins to feel Your love and, as it does, it lets go of all its guilt. It no longer needs to punish itself, for You have healed it. Its coat soon changes to a brilliant white as You continue to whisper, "I love you; I forgive you, for you have been washed in the Blood of the Lamb".

The next lamb, Lord, trembles with fear as You pick her up. She is afraid that You are going to punish her, but no, Lord, You look at her and You call her by name. You call this lamb "Beloved". You gently stroke her and, as You do, her tremors are stilled. You put Your hands over her eyes, Lord, and You wash away the scales that have kept her burdened with guilt, fear and anxiety. As You take Your hands away, the scales begin to fall and this lamb sees with a new light. She sees Your love and the love of the Father.

Now You take time for one last lamb who has just been standing back. It has only been an observer, but it seems to be coming closer now. As You extend Your arms, the lamb shies away so You leave Your place and You walk towards it. You meet in the center of the pasture and You tell this lamb to drop its defenses for it is not necessary to put up walls. You see that the lamb is hesitant to trust you, so You get down on Your knees and You wrap Your arms around its whole body, Lord and You give it time, time to trust You, time to drop all its defenses. Lord, for the first time this lamb becomes honest with You. Your hearts meet; Your spirits meet and the lamb becomes unshackled. In a loving voice, You softly whisper, "By the Blood of the Lamb you have been set free. Your chains have been cut away; you are set free to go".

My Healing
Lord God, how gracious You are to welcome me as Your lamb; how just You are to forgive me with a loving heart. Lord, as I look back over my life I can see that I have worn coats of many colors. There have been times when my coat has been gray, due to the unforgiveness I have harbored within my heart. You have always known this, Lord, and yet with patience and understanding You have waited for my surrender, Oh, how long it has taken me to recognize that harboring unforgiveness brings illness to the body as well as to the soul. Lord, tonight I ask for the Grace to surrender to You my coat of unforgiveness.

Sometimes, Lord, my coat has been black, soiled and stained with guilt, guilt for what I have done, and guilt for what I have failed to do. Oh, how many times You have extended Your Hand, Lord, wanting to give me rest from the weight of my burdens, but I chose to carry this cross rather than to release it to You. Tonight, Lord, I ask for the willingness to shed this coat, giving to You my burden of guilt.

Then there were times, Lord, when my coat was colorless. At those times I seemed to wander around aimlessly, having no purpose or direction in my life. I found my world to be empty and lonely. Oh, if only I could have known that those were the days when You were the closest to me, but in my loneliness I was blinded by self. Tonight, Lord, I ask for the gift of loving others so that, by taking the focus off self, my coat may be restored to a glowing white.

Group Sharing

This meditation was a special gift to all of us, for never before had we experienced such a tremendous release of emotions. For years our lives had been bound by fear, anxiety and guilt, leaving us trapped in a world of our own with no avenue of escape to express ourselves. Now in just a matter of moments our hearts began to open like the clouds in the heavens on a stormy day. As we poured forth our emotions, love began to move throughout the room.

One by one, we entered the pastures through the prayers of one another, These prayers gave each individual the encouragement and the freedom to go forward to meet Jesus. As we each approached the Lord, we began to see ourselves in a new light for we were no longer captives stained and dirty, but now cleansed and freed by the Blood of the Lamb. By the end of the evening we each knew that in the eyes of Jesus we were His lamb, born in the shelter of the Father's wings.

Reflection
"But if we confess our sins to God, he will keep His promises and do what is right: he will forgive us our sins and purify us from our wrongdoing." (1 John 1:9)

HOW IMPORTANT IS GOD'S ARMOR!

Margaret's Meditation

God has made every single provision for us that we could ever need, and one of these provisions is God's armor. In Ephesians the Lord talks about spiritual war. Verse 11 says, "For we wrestle not against flesh and blood, but against principalities, against powers, against the rulers of darkness of this world, against spiritual wickedness in high places." So Scripture is telling us here that each of us is in a spiritual battle, and we need God's armor. We have been given God's armor so that we may be able to resist the devil's tactics, the spiritual army of evil in the heavens. If we don't rely on God's armor we will not be able to resist when the worst happens. We won't have enough resources to stand our ground.

In Ephesians 6:10, it says, "Grow strong in the Lord with the strength of His power." This lets us know that we can't do it on our own; we need God's power. Through baptism He has given us the Holy Spirit who is the power of God. So we do have God's power to resist evil.

It is very important for us to realize that all the evil on earth originates in the kingdom of darkness. It does not originate with God. Many times we will hear people say, "God sent me this cross to bear", and that is simply not the truth. God is all good and all loving. There is nothing bad that comes from God. However God can bring good out of bad circumstances. God does not send sickness into this world; He does not send evil. We must really begin to understand this. Years ago martyrdom was a fact. If we read the Acts of the Apostles we see that Peter and Paul expected to be martyrs, but since so many people today feel they can no longer become martyrs, they have chosen to believe that evil happenings are crosses sent by God. So tonight we are going to become aware of the armor God has given us, so that we can combat the forces of evil.

God has given everything for our protection, and He wants to tells us that we must stand our ground with the truth buckled around our waist, integrity for a breast-plate, wearing for shoes on our feet the eagerness to spread the gospel of peace, and always carrying the shield of faith to put out the burning arrows of evil. We must accept salvation from God to be our helmet and receive the Word of God from the Spirit to use as a sword. Scripture tells us to pray all the time asking for what we need and to pray in the Spirit on every occasion. God has provided a covering for every single part of our body; there is no part that can be exposed to the enemy if we use the armor that He gives us.

So tonight we are going to stand our ground. No matter what situation we find ourselves in, we will no longer retreat before the enemy. We now stand right where we are with the truth buckled around our waist.

The truth is that God loves us, that God is all good, and that God has made every provision for us.

Integrity is our breastplate. Integrity means goodness; it means wholeness; it means a unity of being, a unity of spirit, soul and body. If we come standing before the Lord with integrity for a breastplate that covers our hearts, it covers all our vital organs, and if our soul and our spirit are in line with God's word and God's will then we are in unity. If we are angry, resentful or bitter then we are not in wholeness; we're not in integrity; we're not in unity with God so we are unprotected. We do need that integrity.

We come before God wearing for shoes on our feet the eagerness to spread the gospel of peace. We're all eager to spread the gospel, to talk about the Lord, but how many times do we spread the gospel of unpeacefulness by our words, our actions, a little criticism here or there. We must spread the gospel of peace. These words must sink deep within our spirit.

We must always carry the shield of faith so that we can keep out the burning arrows of the evil one. Faith is realities unseen. So regardless of what the enemy is bringing against us, we must protect ourselves from those burning arrows. We have to hold the shield of faith so none of those arrows slip in. It's not always easy to do this. Some of us have been praying for things for a long time, and we haven't yet seen the answers. It doesn't mean the answer isn't coming; it means that it's just not the time yet. The angel told Daniel that from the moment he prayed God heard his prayer and sent the angel with answer, but the angel was held up by the prince of Persia, who was the evil one. So even God's messengers are held up. Regardless of what we are praying for, we have to hold up that shield of faith. so that the enemy doesn't discourage us from believing that in time we will know God's will.

We must accept salvation from God to be our helmet. A helmet also protects very important organs in our body. When the helmet is put on it protects our brain, our ears; the visor will protect our eyes and the mouthpiece will protect our mouth. A helmet is very essential, and salvation is our helmet. We have accepted Jesus as our Savior, and so we have been saved and we have salvation.

We must receive the Word of God from the Spirit to use as a sword. Notice that everything else we have described has been defensive. It is to cover us, to protect us, to keep us safe, but the sword is the offense. When Jesus was in the desert He was tempted', and each time He answered the enemy with Scripture. Jesus quoted the Old Testament by saying that man does not live by bread alone. He also said that we must not tempt God. So Jesus used the Word of God which is Scripture as His sword against the enemy.

If we really knew Scriptures, we wouldn't get into the problems that we do. We would have an offensive weapon to use against Satan. If Satan comes and tells us that we're sinners, if he's persecuting us, we don't have to feel guilt. We can turn to Scripture in the Psalms and we can say, "God has put our sins as far as the East is from the West", and Satan will have to leave. If Satan says we are supposed to live in poverty, we can go to the Psalms and say, "No, God has promised abundance to all who serve Him." There is an answer in the Word of God for every situation. We must always remember that Jesus is the

Word of God. In John 1, it tells us in the beginning was the Word and the Word was with God and the Word was God. It's not just Scripture; it's Jesus Himself as a person. Revelation tells us that, as the Lamb, He used the double-edged sword and defeated the enemy.

We must pray on every occasions as the Spirit leads, asking for what we need. If we are in a situation where everyone isn't living a Christian life we can pray about it,because Scripture promises us that when we come to the Lord our whole household will come. For some people who find that they can't sleep at night, Scripture says never to get tired of staying awake to pray for all God's people. Many times God awakens us and He uses our prayers for someone who has a real need. Sometimes we hear about it later and sometimes we don't, but nevertheless, someone has a need and God wants us to pray about it.

My Healing
What a wonderful revelation this meditation was for me. In all my travels I don't believe I had ever heard of God's armor and, if I had, it must have been dropped along the roadside. So many times we hear Bible passages but they fall upon deaf ears. It's not that we disbelieve them; it's just that we're not yet ready to receive them. We're not yet ready to experience the depth of their meaning. Now in an instant, like a flash of lightening, my eyes were opened and I was ready to receive God's armor.

With much excitement my mind began to wander back over the years that I had left behind. I now wondered how I could have possibly survived without the

help of God's armor. There were many times in my past
when I could remember encountering struggles with
Satan. Who was protecting me then, or was it just mere
luck that kept me alive? As I continued to meditate, with
my own ears I heard the words of Scripture, "pray
without ceasing", and I knew without a shadow of a doubt
that my parents' prayers throughout my life had been the
instrument that had placed God's armor upon me.

I now realized that I had a job to do, for with growth
comes responsibility both to ourselves as well as others.
I could think of many people who needed the protection
of God's armor, and what a blessing to know that through
my prayers, night or day, I could give this precious gift
away.

Group Sharing
This Scripture opened new avenues of thinking for each
group member. We were all amazed when we considered
the possibility of arriving with little or no protection, yet
returning home with a new coat of armor. That night we
placed God's armor around ourselves as well as our loved
ones. We left Goldweber knowing that we had received a
treasured gift, one that might very well change the
course of our lives.

Reflection
"Put on all the armor that God gives you, so that you will
be able to stand up against the devil's evil tricks."
(Ephesians 6:11).

THE GIFT OF REPENTANCE

One of the first gifts I received from inner healing was the gift of repentance. When this session began I was really unaware of the depth of meaning or the spiritual importance that was placed upon the word "repentance". My only thought on the subject was knowing that it was something one does when feeling sorrowful for sins.

Margaret opened this session by telling us that in order to receive God's unconditional love we should first repent. We must confess our sins and ask for God's forgiveness. She told us that this evening's meditation would lead us to the Cross and that the Holy Spirit would be our guide.

As Margaret began to pray I wondered how I could ever make this journey, for to journey a person must first be free. I had never tasted the joy of freedom for I had always been bound by sins. How could I ever repent in front of all these people anyway? How could I share my experiences with people I barely knew? Besides, repenting would mean weeping and how could weep when I was unable to recognize my own sins? I now wondered if I was even ready to repent, for to repent would mean to look at self, and to look at self would mean: I would see me; the group would see me; even worse, God would see me.

It took quite a while before I persuaded myself to make the journey. By the time I finally got on my way I could see that the group was a great distance ahead of me. Feeling totally alone, I started to panic, but then I remembered that Margaret had prayed for the guidance of the Holy Spirit. Difficult as it was, I tried to imagine the Holy Spirit leading me as I inched my way slowly toward the Cross.

Soon I began to feel very uncomfortable for the sun was hot, my mouth was dry, and the road seemed long and tedious. I was well into my trip when I came upon a bend in the road. This was a welcomed change from the straight and narrow path that I had been following.Somehow this gave me the incentive to go on.

As I rounded the bend I could see that there was a sign ahead of me. Although I was unable to read it. I found that it aroused my curiosity and so I pressed forward. Much to my disappointment, when I approached the sign I read the words "Rough Road Ahead". What was I to do now, for I was already much too tired. I wondered if I turned back would I reach Goldweber before dark. I had always been afraid of the dark, so I certainly didn't want to be on this trail alone, after dark. Oh, how could I ever make the right decision. Once again I had to stop and remind myself that I was not alone, for the Holy Spirit was still leading me. I also realized that not one group member had turned back. With this in mind I continued on.

Before long I found myself walking on a road filled with pebbles. This not only slowed me down but it caused a great deal of discomfort to the soles of my feet. By now the weight of my burdens was beginning to lay heavily upon my shoulders, and each step that I took seemed endless. I knew that what I needed was some encouragement, so I began to center my thoughts upon Christ. What was His walk to Calvary like? He carried the sins of the whole world upon His shoulders and the weight of His burdens must have been unbearable. Now mine seemed so insignificant.

As I continued to walk, I asked myself if this trip was being made in vain. What good could possibly come out of all this struggle? Was I really ready to be honest with myself as well as with God? Was I willing to surrender my pride in order to receive repentance? How could I ever find any humility in a heart that had turned so cold?

Now fear was beginning to settle in, for I was unsure of what I was able to give up, and just as unsure of what God would be asking of me. At the cross, Christ had given up everything including His cloak, but He was God, and I was just a sinner. Why should I have to part with everything? I realized that negativity was starting to fill my path, and if I was ever to complete this journey I must focus on the positive rather than the negative. I had to admit there had been signs of hope along the way, for I had now begun to recognize the importance of faith. I was indeed taking each step by faith, not knowing the outcome, but somehow trusting in His promise that through repentance comes forgiveness.

As I rounded the next bend I came to a fork in the road. There was a huge sign with two arrows, one pointing to the left saying "One Way", the other pointing to the right and saying "Free Way". I chose the sign "One Way", for I had been on a freeway all my life and it had led me nowhere. Now I knew there was no turning back for me, for I had made my choice and my decision must stand, I then thought of the time that perhaps Christ might have wanted to turn back, especially knowing that He faced death at the end of His journey. He too, must have tasted fear but yet He carried on. I must do the same.

I must have walked for miles before I spotted my next landmark. This was a large boulder in the middle of the road. The words written on it were "Come all ye who are heavy laden and I will give you rest". My heart began to leap for at that moment I wanted to believe that this sign was one that included me.

As I drew nearer to my destination I once again was able to see the group. I noticed that they were all weeping as they walked. Oh how I envied their tears, for tears were not something that came easily for me. I was so delighted to have them in my view again, for throughout the trip I was concerned that they would arrive without me. By now the trip had taken its toll of me. I was exhausted and no longer worried about what they might think. My only desire was to mingle among the crowd, hoping that God wouldn't notice me. He surely must have known my thoughts for His timing was perfect. Impossible as it may seen, we all arrived together. Side by side, we stood at the foot of the Cross. As Margaret played the song, "We're Standing on Holy Ground", we knelt before our God.

Then like a child waiting to be chastized, I heard myself utter the words, "Father, forgive me". What transpired in those next few moments was indeed a miracle, for as I reached up to embrace the Cross the joy of heaven touched my life. A peace that surpasseth all understanding began to flood my soul as God's love showered down upon me. Realizing that there were no limitations to His forgiveness, I rose and stepped forward to receive His love. In those remaining moments the death and resurrection of Christ took on new meaning, for I knew that He had no longer come just for others; He had also come for me.

Through this experience I was able to see that my own resurrection had begun, for God had heard my plea and shown His mercy on me. As I drove home that night new revelations began to surface one by one:

- Repentance is a gift of God's grace, not some thing to be feared.

- God came for sinners; we do not have to hide among the crowd.

- The weight of sin is heavy when carried alone.

- Humility is not something we have to search for when we stand before our Maker.

- Repentance brings reconciliation with the Father.

- Repentance brings God's kingdom to us.

- Repentance can change our lives, for it has changed mine.

- Repentance is the gateway to our own resurrection.

Repentance for me was a time of feeling rather than a time of talking. When we repent there are few words to say, for the act itself says it all. In order to find God, repentance must become our daily walk. I pray that I shall always remember that long, tedious journey from Goldweber to the Cross!

Reflection

"There will be more joy in heaven over one sinner who repents than over ninety-nine respectable people who do not need to repent. . . . I tell you, the angels of God rejoice over one sinner who repents." (Luke 15:7, 10).

THE GIFT OF FRIENDSHIP

I have searched all my life for a very special friendship, one with qualities of love, compassion and much understanding. I have had many good friends on my path, but somehow they have never been able to fulfill my needs. Oh,it's not that they haven't tried, for each in his own way has given to me a gift of God's love. Yet I still thirst for a deep and lasting friendship. After many years of searching I have asked myself just what is it that I am seeking in a friendship, and is it within my reach or is it an impossible dream.

I wonder why it is that we're so selective in some areas of our lives and not in others. I often notice people doing their shopping in a busy supermarket. It doesn't seem to matter how crowded the aisles become or how many times they must push their carts from side to side. Their only real concern is being very selective in choosing the product they are purchasing. How carefully they examine each item by the pounds, ounces, size and price. Their time and effort put forth into shopping never ceases to amaze me.

Why is it that we fail to put forth as much time and effort into selecting our friends as we do into our shopping? Is it because we underestimate the true value of a meaningful friendship? Perhaps this is why we seldom find in each other what we find in that one selective item in a busy shopping center. The word, I believe, is quality. When people go to a thrift store they're looking for a second hand bargain, but when they go to a shopping mall they want the best their money can buy. In a way friendship is a lot like shopping, for most often we get out of it just what we put into it.

Friendship like every other commitment carries with it a measure of responsibility, so we do have a right to be selective. There are many factors that must be taken into consideration. One might be our location; perhaps there aren't a lot of people in the area in which we live. Another might be our age; most of us feel more comfortable being around people our own age. Then there is the avenue of interest, for if we have nothing in common, how can we cultivate a friendship? Lifestyles must be considered; single people may find it almost impossible relating to someone who has been married for a life time. Religion is also a very important issue; unless we find a spiritual bond there may always be a degree of conflict.

Another factor may well be our past. I'm sure, like myself, most of you have experienced at one time or another the disappointments of friendships. These past disappointments can affect our choices of friends today. Most often we find ourselves avoiding people who remind us of those unpleasant memories. Those memories seem to leave us with much distrust, limiting our selection when considering new friendships. So, I have found that being selective is not an easy task, but it is certainly one of the first steps towards building a friendship.

What makes a quality friendship anyway, and are we capable of sharing one with each other? I believe, in order to find the answers we're searching for, we must reflect back on our own personal experiences. Have our friendships been rooted in honesty? How often in life we desire to tell others how we really feel, but we neglect to do so in fear of hurting them. Many times their responses to insignificant issues teach us to skirt around more important issues, those that might spark defensivemess or intimidation. Little do we realize that in trying to shield them from hurting we often prevent them from growing. Failure to be honest with another usually results in resentment within ourselves, and this eventually hinders our own growth. We must recognize that growth comes from our experiences, and hurting is sometimes one of them.

Being responsible is another quality that we often overlook. Many of us desire the pleasures of friendship but not the obligations that go along with it. Being committed is a sacrifice, one in which we concern ourselves with the health, well being and growth of each other. We learn that friendship is not merely a phone call once in awhile, for that is nothing more than an acquaintance. If we truly want to grow together in God's love, then we must make time for one another.

Trust is also a quality that makes friendship so special. How often we are entrusted with someone's innermost secrets and we are expected to keep them private. Promises are made; intentions are good, but time and again we fall short of our goal.

Loyalty is another fine quality. Are we loyal in our bond to each other? Friendship often breeds jealousy from outsiders. Their mission is gossip; their words are deceptive. How quickly we find ourselves influenced by their destructive criticism.

Forgiveness is a quality that must become a part of us in order to develop a loving friendship. Sometimes we tend to hold each other accountable for our various mistakes. In our humanness we seem quick to judge and slow to forgive. A lasting friendship can only be maintained through the quality of forgiveness. Acceptance is one more important quality. How often we find ourselves trying to control the behavior and choices in the life of another. We give little thought to the feelings and experiences that have shaped the path they have taken. Believing that our choices would be suitable, we try to impose our will upon them. There comes a time when we must all let go, for acceptance is a part of letting go. Only when we give them the encouragement to seek God's will, will they be free to make the right choices for their lives.

Thinking of all the qualities that friendship should embrace, I came to realize that neither I nor anyone else could possibly be the perfect friend. Yet in my quest for love I continued to search. Then one night through the gift of Inner Healing I received the answer I was looking for.

It was the beginning of the evening and Margaret once again opened the session by evoking the guidance of the Holy Spirit. This was no longer unusual for us, for this prayer had become our way of life. What was unusual though was that this time I heard it with my heart instead of my ears. What a grace to discover that during all those many months of praying, "Come, Holy Spirit", God was actually planting a seed. For the life-long friend that I had been seeking was the Holy Spirit living within me. In the moments that followed a miracle took place; God opened my heart to the workings of His Spirit. As we broke bread together in friendship, my soul was touched with wisdom.

Who else could give to us all the qualities we so desire to find in one another? Who else could teach us how to love? The Holy Spirit can share our moments of joy and comfort us in our sorrow. In times of trouble we can depend on His guidance. Within His trust we can place our secrets, for when we need to talk His Heart is always listening. He does not criticize, nor does He judge. He does not control nor does He possess. He's never selfish, and He never demands. In our lonliness He is present; in our sadness He brings cheer. When we need encouragement He gives hope, and when we're in doubt He waits with us. In our decisions He gives us confidence; in our growth He gives us insight. When we succeed He shares our happiness; when we fail He shares our tears. He heals our broken hearts and mends our broken dreams. His honesty is immeasureable; His wisdom is total grace. His forgiveness is unending; His love is infinite.

This session on love has taught me many wonderful things. True friendship is not an impossible dream. If we can shop for the best product that money can buy, then we can select the best friendship that love can create. It's true the Holy Spirit is the only perfect friend but if we allow Him to develop the hidden qualities within us, then perhaps we can each give to one another what we so desire for ourselves.

Today I know that I was the bargain hunter, and my friends the quality shoppers, receiving much less than they had given. I've learned that in order to maintain lasting friendships, we must first put forth the effort to enrich the qualities of our own hearts; for friendship is a treasured gift and we must do our part to make it a blessing. Always remember that each friendship nurtured by the Holy Spirit will grow into a seed of love.

Reflection

"Love never gives up; and its faith, hope, and patience never fail." (1 Corinthians 13:7)

HEALING THE STONY HEART

"For I will take you from among the Gentiles and gather you together from all the countries and will bring you into your own land. And I will pour upon you clean water, and you shall be cleansed from all your filthiness, and I shall cleanse you from all your idols. I will give you a new heart, and put a new spirit within you: and I will take away the stony heart out of your flesh, and give you a heart of flesh. And I will put my spirit in the midst of you and cause you to walk in my commandments and to keep my judgements and do them." (Ezekiel 36:24-27 *Duay Version, Challoner Revision*)

In the first part of this scripture the Lord says He is bringing us to our own land, which is back home with Him. Then He says He will pour clean water over us and cleanse us from all our filthiness which is our sins. and then from all our idols. These idols can be money, family, friendships— anything that comes ahead of Him. Then

He says He is going to remove our hearts of stone and give us new hearts of flesh.

Did you ever wonder what causes us to harden our hearts? Isn't it true that out of protection we harden our hearts so that we won't get hurt anymore? A heart of stone is really a heart of protection; it's our defense, whereas a heart of flesh is a vulnerable heart, one that is always exposed. Then the Lord says, "I shall put my spirit in you and make you keep my laws and sincerely respect my observances." This I believe is the promise. If we have the heart of flesh we will receive the Spirit.

Margaret's Meditation
Father, You have told us in Your Word that if today we hear Your voice, to harden not our hearts. Lord, we ask You now to walk us back in time, to that time when we were first so wounded that we started to harden our hearts. Just show us Lord that place where we unconsciously and instinctively began to harden our hearts. Lord bring Your Son Jesus, our Healer, our Redeemer, into that moment, that moment of attack, that moment of misunderstanding, that moment when we were so fearful and so frightened that we began to harden our hearts. Just send your Son into that moment Lord and let us see Jesus coming. Let the light of His presence light the darkness for each of us.. Come, Lord Jesus, come in a ray of light, a ray of hope. Let the light of Your love reflect upon us and our woundedness. Help us tonight, Lord Jesus, to be healed.

Lord, I see a little girl hiding in the closet. She doesn't know that she did wrong; she just knows that her mother is angry. She knows that her mother is looking for her so, out of fear, she runs and hides in the closet. She's so still, Lord; she doesn't move. She's afraid to make a sound. She's so, so still.

She hears someone approaching the closet and she's in fear that her mother will open that door. She hides her head, Lord; she puts her head down on her knees and she gets all curled up. The door opens softly now and the little girl just waits in fear, but there's not a sound. Nothing seems to be happening and she doesn't understand. She turns her head towards the door and as she begins to open her eyes she realizes the closet is not dark anymore. There's a soft shiny light; it's not harsh and it's not bright. It's just very soft and very warm. This little girl feels all that warmth, all that light. As she lifts her head a little more she opens her eyes and she sees You, Lord, standing there. You fill up the whole doorway with Your light, There's such a beautiful expression on Your face Lord. It is such a compassionate face. Your love radiates from your eyes, Jesus.

As You reach out Your hand You gesture for her to come. She's still fearful for You're so tall to a little girl. So You just bend down and You kneel on the floor of the closet. You just kneel beside her Lord and You wait. You give her time to become comfortable with You, time for her fear and her anxieties to fall away in the light of Your love. After a while she becomes trusting in Your presence, so she inches closer to You, closer and closer, Lord, and then finally she takes Your hand.

As your hands meet, she feels Your love flow through her body. It flows through her with such a warmth, Lord, that it melts away the ice around her tiny heart, that wounded and fearful heart. Your healing warmth flows into that wounded heart and she feels so relaxed, so comfortable. She feels so loved. Your love is like an energy flowing through her, releasing all her pain, all her fears. This energy flows through her whole body, through her mind, through her emotions. All the tension fades away, and then Lord you stand together and the two of you leave the closet.

You go back into the room and you sit down together. There's an airiness about the room that didn't seem to be there in the closet. It's like a fresh breath, a fresh spirit. she leans back and relaxes Lord as You hold her against Your chest. As she basks in the warmth of Your love You tell her it's time to go to the Father. Now Lord it's no longer a little girl traveling with You but an adult with a stone around her heart. It's like a chain wrapped around her used as a shield to protect her from any woundedness, any rejection. As you walk hand in hand you continue on your journey.

The Lord begins to remind us now of all those times we have sinned, and all those times we were sinned against. Each in turn added a stone, and each stone built the stony wall around our hearts. Jesus points out to us now those times of misunderstanding, those sins, and we repent. As we become more willing to be vulnerable, to understand other people's woundedness, those people who sinned against us, the stones begin to fall from our hearts.

Now the Lord brings us to the throne room of our Father and outside that throne room is another little room. It's a marble room and there's a table there with a beautiful crystal bowl. It's a very large bowl, large enough for the Lord to stand up in the center of it. He holds in His hand a beautiful crystal jug filled with clear sparkling water. He calls us to stand in the center of the bowl with Him. Soon He begins to pour this refreshing water over us. It's not too hot and it's not too cold; it just refreshes us and frees us. He pours it over our heads and it runs down our hair. It runs down our forehead, over our eyebrows, over our cheeks. It runs down our back and over our arms. It covers us completely. The Lord keeps pouring until we are completely cleansed, and He says to us, "I will pour clean water over you, I will restore you, I will refresh you."

Mary is standing there now with a beautiful velvet towel in her hands. She wraps it around us and wipes the water from our faces. We have tears streaming from our eyes and so she wipes them away. She begins to dry our hair and then our hands. She kneels down now to dry our feet. She wants to caress them for she sees they're wounded from the strange paths we have taken, paths filled with rocky stones and sharp branches. So she tends to our feet for there's healing in her hands.

Soon the bruises begin to disappear and the wounds become healed. Then she gives us a garment. It's a soft garment and very beautiful. She just slips it over our heads and helps us to put our arms through it. She straightens the folds, puts our hair in place and then she turns to Jesus, "My Son this child, who was lost and You rescued, is now ready." With Jesus on our right and Mary on our left, they take us to the Father.

The Father is sitting in a rocking chair facing the door. He's expecting us to come. Our angels went before us telling the Father that at last we were coming home. At last our hearts of stone had been removed. Now cleansed of all defilement we could rightly enter into His presence.

The Father reaches out and beckons us to come closer. Our desire is to fall at His feet but Mary says, "No, this is not the time." So we remain standing as the Father takes from a table a brand new heart. It is breathtaking as we look at it for it is so beautiful, and it is so alive. Then He hands it to Jesus and Jesus with His gentle touch enters and places the heart within us. It is such a vulnerable heart, opened and flowing with love, compassion and understanding.

Now we are truly rightful children of His, for the promise has been fulfilled. We have new life in Jesus, and the Father, through the power of the Spirit. The wounds of our past have been cleansed and healed. As we turn to leave the Father says, "Stay awhile and rest in My love, absorb all I have to give you. Then go forth in My name to the emotionally wounded. Attest to My love, so that they too can be restored to me."

My Healing

This was a very moving experience for me— a heart wounded by sin, a heart bruised by others, a wall built so high no one could get over it, and so deep that no one could get under it. There were no flowers growing around my wall, for the only seed planted became a bitter root.

It's difficult to understand how a child's heart changes its course in youth, but sometimes it does. Perhaps this is for protection, perhaps for survival. Nevertheless it happens. Before I knew it I was a teenager and those around me a target. As the years passed the roots grew deeper, each one flourishing in the soil of resentment.

During this meditation I wondered why Jesus had

taken so long to visit the heart of a child. Hadn't He ever heard my prayers? I pondered these thoughts with great depth, until I discovered that Jesus had visited me many times before. The child was always willing; the adult was always angry. To receive a heart of flesh, I had to dissolve my heart of stone. This was done only through the gift of forgiveness. I've learned that becoming whole is a long journey, but it is possible if we learn to forgive one another. Today my heart is a vulnerable heart, fed by the Father's love, nourished by the power of the Spirit.

Group Sharing
Before this meditation started we were each asked to pray, and then to select a stone representing our heart. I believe everyone knew the importance of this session from the moment it began. It would be profound; it would be revealing, but most of all vital to our spiritual growth.

There was a great deal of emotion being shown throughout this meditation, so most of us were quite drained when it was over. Our group sharing led to the expression of many hidden feelings. For some the stony heart was a time of isolation, being alone and cut off from those they loved. One person said it had narrowed her vision and limited her communication with others. Another explained her feelings of self rightousness, and how she had justified her stony heart. Being on the defensive had given them an excuse to retaliate. One man described it as a dried cinder, dark with no love. Margaret portrayed it as "heart of flesh, source of life". She added that in a stony heart life is not present.

Margaret as well as the group members knew that this meditation was the beginning of new life, but indeed only the beginning. For most of us it had taken years to build our stony hearts. Now it would take the Lord, time, tears, and much willingness to let go, and accept our new hearts of flesh.

Reflection

". . . I shall remove the heart of stone from your bodies and give you a heart of flesh instead." (Ezekiel 36:26, *The New Jerusalem Bible*. New York: Doubleday,1985.)

PRAYER TO THE BLESSED MOTHER

When I was a child, Mary, to me you were a mystery; as an adult, I have found you to be a miracle.

I still can recall that joyous December when I asked my parents to make my gift a statue of you. How beautiful you were when you appeared under our tree that Christmas morning! For a while, Mary, our relationship became really special for there was something within me that drew me to you. Perhaps it was your grace, or perhaps it was your warmth when I gazed upon your lovely face. Whatever the reason, you stirred my spirit and so I took you for my very own.

In those days I traveled a lot, Mary, so you became my companion. Wherever I went you went; wherever I dwelled you were placed where all could see you when they entered my household. You were seldom the topic of conversation, Mary, but I knew you were there, protecting me and those I loved.

Then one night due to the abuse of alcohol, someone broke your statue into a million pieces. This was a moment I would never want to relive for my heart was truly broken. From that day forward, whenever I passed your empty table I hurt a little bit more. Eventually I moved away, Mary, only this time you were no longer beside me. I cannot recall if I ever actually prayed to you then, but if I did those prayers must have ceased. There was much turmoil to come upon my path and during those troubled times my feelings for you were forgotten.

Years later in the Lamb of God prayer community, you entered my life once again. I remember that night so vividly, Mary. There was a speaker there from Staten Island; his name was Jerry Kelly. At the end of the evening he said individual prayers for all who desired them. As I stood before the Blessed Sacrament this man dedicated my life to you, Mary, as your child and a child of God. In the silence of those moments I was received into your hands. There was no containing the waves of grace that echoed from your love.

Now you were no longer a statue but a living presence that had enfolded me. This was the first time, Mary, I had ever experienced the true meaning of Holy Ground. Before Jerry ended his prayer he applied a scripture to me, "Stop hiding your light under a bushel basket."* he said. Since that night, Mary, you have become a very important part of my life; our bond has been rekindled. Our togetherness has made me recognize time and again that I am your child, and that through your love for me, my light for Jesus will shine.

In recent years, Mary, you have taught me some wonderful things about myself. How vividly I remember a celebration of your Immaculate Conception. I was at

---

*Adapted from Matt 5:15.

mass and once again sitting in front of the Blessed Sacrament. It was one of those times, Mary, when I was at my lowest ebb, and you appeared before me. Your garment was pure white and your beauty was breathtaking. Little did I know then what you came to tell me, for you chose not to speak. As you stood in silence I waited patiently for a sign or a word, but I received nothing. Then all of a sudden within my spirit I discovered that your image was the word, for you were the message that God was sending to me. Although I was unable to fully discern your message that night, Mary, for that took much grace and spiritual direction, in time I understood the true meaning of your mission.

All my life, Mary, I have struggled with the female within me, always trying to live as one yet never really wanting to be one. Since childhood, being a female has always represented something unclean to me. That feeling never seemed to be there when I looked at other females, but always when I looked within myself. Your image, Mary, was to show me that living the life of a female was God's true desire for me. Your garment of white was to represent purity as well as beauty within the life of a female. Today, Mary, on occasion I still have that re- occuring sense of being dirty, but when I do I look to you, a female, the mother of God. Then I receive your peace.

O Blessed Mother, the road to inner healing has been most difficult for each of us, but your presence in our group has made it possible to continue on our journey. Many nights during our sessions, Mary, you have made yourself known in prophecy, speaking often through the gift of tongues. However, sometimes you have come in the wake of a whisper, your message unspoken yet penetrating into the depths of our hearts. Your strength and encouragement, Mary, have always given us the incentive to look deep within ourselves. How often we have needed your assistance as we traveled back into those painful memories of childhood. You, Mary, have been our catalyst in the healing of so many relationships, especially those involving our mothers. It seems as if their love has been the root of a new beginning for most of us. How far we've come since those days of separation, those days when feelings of rejection and little self worth seemed to control our lives. How often as children we reached out for that unattainable love, perhaps almost given, yet never quite received.

Your continual visits to us Mary, as mother, have provided us with the many loving insights needed to see beyond a child's vision. One of those insights was finding out that some of us never really knew the true meaning of love, as it relates to mothers. How quick we were to judge them; how slow we were to listen. As children we were certainly incapable of understanding, but as adults, now living in a world where abortions are acceptable to many, you have taught us each, Mary, a valuable lesson. That unattainable love that we so often desired was but a moment in time, for the true love of a mother is the decision and sacrifice she makes to keep, to shelter, to feed, clothe and raise her child. This is the gift of life; no greater love could a mother give.

Your presence in our lives. Mary, has taught us how to bridge the gap between mother and self. Through your grace we have been reunited. Our relationships are now ongoing, for some on earth, for some in heaven. Today we each know that the fruit of our own mother's womb bore a miracle. We are those miracles.

How extraordinary this journey has been, Mary, with you by our side. It has been your love that has inspired us to go forward. At times our emotional paths have seemed impossible to travel, but your light has penetrated far beyond our realm of reasoning.

How often you have been there to greet us with a gentle touch and an understanding heart. Pure love has been your response to our human imperfections, your arms always extended, your mantle a protective covering — a mission with one purpose only, to lead your children to your beloved Son. Yes, Mary, you are our Lady of Liberty. You have guided us through troubled waters; by your light of freedom you have led us to your harbor. Blessed Mother, in our meditations we have scaled your mountaintop; together we have stood at the foot of your Son's cross, for some only a vision, for others a reality. Many have seen your sun rise and set on Medjugorje; we have seen your Son rise and set on Goldweber.

Reflection
"And Mary said, 'My soul doth magnify the Lord . . . for, behold, from henceforth all generations shall call me blessed.'" (Luke"1:46,48 *Authorized King James Version*)

PART THREE

THE PRAYERFUL SHEPHERD

While I was participating in Inner Healing, my journey to wholeness needed the additional help of counseling and later on, of Spiritual Direction. Margaret alerted me to these needs. God provided for them through the pastor of the Church of Saint Veronica in Howell, New Jersey. Through, this "Prayerful Shepherd", Christ carried me through a very difficult phase of my journey and set me on a path to a deeper and more intimate relationship with Him.

The Bible does not specifically mention Saint Veronica, but according to a tradition, while others were jeering and reviling a condemned, cross-burdened Christ, she courageously offered Him her veil to wipe His brow. When Jesus returned it to her, it bore His image.

COUNSELING

A year after I joined inner healing Margaret suggested that, due to my deep-seated problems, I should seek professional counseling. She explained to me that there were many issues to deal with that really needed the advice and prayers of a priest and that in some of these areas I required more help than she could offer. She said that priests were given special graces so through her encouragement I sought the help of Father Brendon Williams, pastor of St. Veronica's Church in Howell, N.J.

In the beginning I was apprehensive for, with the exception of a few healing masses, I had had no previous contact with Father. I had never before shared my story with a stranger so I was quite concerned about his response. In the first few sessions I shared only bits and pieces of my life. After awhile when I was feeling more comfortable with him, I was able to express some of those deep-seated problems. Soon the counseling was enabling me to release my troubled emotions and so I started anticipating each visit.

When Father felt the time was right we began to focus on my immediate problems. Now the sessions took on a new format. First I would explain the problem I was having. Usually it would be something from my past that was beginning to surface. Then Father would take me on a journey of prayer back to those moments of yesterday, often to a place where I would experience tremendous pain, a place where throughout the years thoughts had been kept well hidden for my own protection. Now in a spirit of prayer, Father and I together would enter into that pain.

Although the journey was fearful, he led me gently into troubled waters. Once inside the eye of the storm, Father's gifts always became manifested. His love and compassion led me to explore depths that I had never before reached, taking me to the heart of each problem. This brought a sense of release, a feeling of freedom, a cleansing from within.

There were often tears, sometimes in sorrow for the things I would have to surrender and sometimes in joy for the things I would discover. Each emotion that I experienced nourished new growth.

During my sessions we touched on wounded areas of my life which included family relationships, sexuality, lifestyles and personal conflicts. With Father's help I was able to develop insight into my own feelings and into the root cause of these troubled areas.

In counseling Father's skills and prayers have helped remove many deep emotional blocks, enabling me to become more receptive to inner healing.

PART THREE CHAPTER TWO

SPIRITUAL DIRECTION

After I had been eighteen months in counseling, Margaret felt it was time for me to seek spiritual direction. Again, her recommendation was Father Brendon Williams. I considered Father's "Yes." a real honor for few people whom I knew had the privilege of a Director. This was perhaps a bit of an ego trip for me, but quickly deflated when I learned that spiritual direction is not an easy task.

Unlike counseling there was much homework to be done, such as daily repentance, prayers, scripture readings, meditations, reflecting on growth and logging events. Counseling for me had been a discovery of self through my own life experiences, but these sessions would no longer focus upon me but upon my relationship with God. This would be a time of emptying self and learning how to bring God into the center of my life.

This would require much discipline. However I was blessed for Father had the endowment of understanding, knowing that few in life learn the art of self- discipline.

Father was always prudent when dealing with my feelings. He often needed to be firm with me but he always had a gentle way of expressing himself. There were times when he had to structure the sessions, especially in the beginning when I wanted every door to open at once. Then he'd have to slow me down, teaching me that growth from spiritual direction was a long time process.

Although trained in pastoral counseling, Father had qualities that went far beyond the realm of study. Each of his gifts were used in perfect timing, according to God's plan. He always knew when to explore, when to guide, when to encourage. His interpretation of prayer took me to the core of my very being, sometimes making me aware of God's presence and sometimes bringing me directly into God's presence.

Father knew in each session when to talk and when to silence himself so that Jesus could speak directly to me. He set no limits on what God could do for me through prayer. His prayers always brought a healing, opened a channel, removed a block or shed discernment on some shadowed area.

Often when Father prayed with me I would see myself as a child, half black and half white, in a casket. Other times I would see the Cross and the Nativity. Later the Virgin Mother revealed that the image of a black and white child represented my struggles between the male and female within me. I explained this to Father. He then prayed with me for the voices of the male to be stilled and for the male to leave my body. He interpreted my image of the Cross to mean not only dying to self but also dying to the male. He interpreted my image of the Nativity to represent new life and the birth of the female within me.

This was indeed a powerful prayer bringing a remarkable healing.* For the first time I could stand before God as the person He created me to be.

In the years I have been with Father, I have made various commitments to myself. These have included attending first Friday mass, saying the Passion for a year, taking spiritual communion and recently reciting the daily rosary. At times, I found it difficult to keep these commitments, but God has given me the grace to persevere. Each one has drawn me closer to Him.

Today Father and I are focusing on contemplative prayer. This is a prayer where one stills the mind, the body and the spirit. It becomes a peaceful state and one, I believe, of supreme grace. It is here in this silence that I turn my face towards God; it is here in these moments that God speaks to me. It is here that I experience the indwelling presence of the Holy Trinity.

It would be difficult to say where counseling stops and spiritual direction begins, but for me they are interwoven by the threads of God's love. Both experiences have been a journey in prayer, leading me into a close personal relationship with our Lord Jesus Christ. Do I know Jesus today? Indeed I do. I found Him in counseling; I found Him in spiritual direction; I found Him in the heart of an Irish priest.

---

*Homosexuals who wish to locate Christian-oriented professional assistance to help them through the conflict between their inclinations and beliefs or who merely desire the spiritual companionship of souls engaged in the same turbulent struggle are invited to call Courage, St. Michael's Rectory, 424 West 34th Street, New York, NY 10001, Telephone (212) 421-0426.

Reflection

"After all, who is Apollos and who is Paul? No more than servants through whom you came to believe . . . I [Paul] may have done the planting, and Apollos the watering, but God made the seed grow!" (1 Corinthians 3:5,6 J. B. Phillips, translator,*The New Testament in Modern English,* Revised Edition, New York: Macmillan, 1972.

RESOURCES

A seminar by Reverend Matthew Linn S.J. and, his brother, Dennis Linn, provided the model and inspiration for the Goldweber Avenue Inner Healing sessions herein described. These facilitators explain the applications, theological roots, and interdisciplinary anchorings of Inner Healing, in a number of publications, including the following books published by Paulist Press:

* *Healing of Memories.*
* *Healing Life's Hurts.*
* *Deliverance Prayer.*

And together with Sheila Fabricant, M. Div. (Now Sheila Linn) :

* *Prayer Course for Healing Life's Hurts.*
* *Praying with Another for Healing.*
* *Healing the Eight Stages of Life.*
* *Belonging: Healing & 12 Step Recovery.*

Ask for them at your bookstore.